THE GOOD FOOD

THE
GOOD FOOD

A Cookbook of Soups, Stews, and Pastas

DANIEL HALPERN
AND JULIE STRAND

ecco

An Imprint of HarperCollins*Publishers*

For Jeanne and Mark

HarperCollins books may be purchased for educational, business, or sales promotional use. For information, please email the Special Markets Department at SPsales@harpercollins.com.

First hardcover edition published in 1985 by Viking Press.

Grateful acknowledgment is made to the following for permission to reprint copyrighted material from other sources:

Harper & Row, Publishers, Inc., and Lescher & Lescher, Ltd.: "Harira" and "Lamb Tagine with Lemons and Olives," from *Couscous and Other Good Food from Morocco,* by Paula Wolfert. Copyright © 1973 by Paula Wolfert.

Holt, Rinehart and Winston, Publishers: "Coq au Vin," from *Michael Field's Cooking School,* by Michael Field. Copyright © 1965 by Michael Field.

Alfred A. Knopf, Inc.: "Boeuf Bourguignon," from *Julia Child's Kitchen,* by Julia Child. Copyright © 1975 by Julia Child. "Paella à la Valenciana," from *The Foods and Wines of Spain,* by Penelope Casas. Copyright © 1979, 1980, 1981, 1982 by Penelope Casas.

Alfred A. Knopf, Inc., and A. M. Heath & Company Ltd.: "Penne with Cauliflower, Garlic and Oil," from *More Classic Italian Cooking,* by Marcella Hazan. Copyright © 1978 by Marcella Hazan and Victor Hazan.

William Morrow & Company, Inc.: "Murgh Masala," from *Classic Indian Cooking,* by Julie Sahni. Copyright © 1980 by Julie Sahni.

Workman Publishing: "Winter Pork and Fruit Ragout" (originally "The Winter Ragu"), from *The Silver Palate Cookbook,* by Julee Rosso and Sheila Lukins. Copyright © 1982 by Julee Rosso and Sheila Lukins. Reprinted with permission of the publisher.

Line drawings by Susan J. Walp. Copyright © 1985 by Susan J. Walp, 1985.

Designed by Suet Yee Chong

Library of Congress Cataloging-in-Publication Data has been applied for.

ISBN 978-0-06-287969-1

19 20 21 22 23 LSC 10 9 8 7 6 5 4 3 2 1

Eating is touch carried to the bitter end.

—SAMUEL BUTLER II

CONTENTS

STEWS

PASTAS

ACCOMPANIMENTS

PREFACE TO THE NEW EDITION

I stand behind Samuel Butler's epigraph to this book: "Eating is touch carried to the bitter end." Although Julie Strand and I wrote *The Good Food* more than thirty years ago, there have been very few meals in my kitchen these past many years that haven't employed recipes from it. Yes, the recipes may seem dated, and I've done nothing to update beyond repairing a few foolish misdirections—and agreeing to two global replacements: begrudgingly, "fresh coriander" to "cilantro" and, happily, "dried Italian mushrooms" to "dried porcini mushrooms." They have to be porcini in my book. And, yes, there is enough heavy cream running through these pages to float a battleship—in the eighties, we thickened soup with heavy cream and egg yolks, always with the proviso that if the liquid boiled, you would be serving breakfast. We have unapologetically left in every tablespoon of heavy cream. There are worse things that we consume.

Many of the ingredients used here were not in stores back then. Depending on where you lived, you had to go to specialty shops—Indian, Mexican, Middle Eastern, Italian, and Chinese—to find items easily purchased today, such as cilantro, cardamom, some of the more exotic brown spices, harissa, tahini, filé powder, fermented black beans, balsamic vinegar, cotechino, and jarred anchovies.

It goes without saying that there are numerous international recipes in *The Good Food*. I learned what I know about cooking mostly in Morocco and Italy, and have always been interested in new and unusual dishes from around the world. My current favorite is a Korean dish called budae-jjigae (army base stew), a dish *not* for those concerned about heavy cream.

I have favorites in this book—as my friend the Cardinal president of the Vatican once told me, "God loves all his children. He loves some more than others." I'll limit myself to a list of five favorites: Mushroom Soup; Harira; Cold Curried Tomato Soup with Mint; Lamb Stew with Eggplant, Saffron, and Ginger; Chicken Tagine with Prunes, Onions, and Almonds; Bobotie; Penne with Cauliflower, Garlic, and Oil; Risotto with Four Cheeses; and the last recipe in the book, the odd Bistro Appetizer. I'm aware that's nine.

But I stand behind all of the recipes, understanding that some have withstood the test of time better than others, to clang a cliché. I love clichés almost as much as heavy cream and fresh cilantro. As the poet and avid gastrolater Charles Simic once wrote, "The dream of every honest cliché is to find its way into a great poem." If there turn out to be clichés in this book, at least they'll taste good.

Regarding the notion of two amateurs imagining we could write a cookbook. Our dinner parties were grand events, or so they seemed then, and actually seem now. The guests, toward the end of dessert, would inevitably raise what was left of their wineglasses, and say in unison: "You must write a cookbook." And so we did. The first ten recipes were a breeze, in and out of the oven, if that's not a mixed metaphor. The next eighty not so much. That said, we did learn something, if only about how to write a first cookbook—and, most important, we realized by the end of the process that we would not write another.

Not to name-drop, but when our copyedited manuscript was returned to us with queries, I understood we were in trouble. There was a yellow Post-it stuck to the first stew recipe. It read: "Why dry the meat before browning it, is it wet?" So I called James Beard to get his advice. He gave me his personal copyeditor. The luck of beginners!

Anyway, I hope these recipes do what recipes should always do: help you eat better.

—Daniel Halpern, New York City, 2018

INTRODUCTION

This collection of recipes is meant to be a celebration of soups, stews, and pastas. We chose these categories because they are the foods we find the most pleasurable to prepare and eat—the foods that seem to be, in some primal way, "the good food"—and we could find no single collection that gathered together an interesting assortment of recipes for these dishes.

The Good Food is, in a sense, an anthology of our own particular tastes, gathered from a variety of sources, a catalog of dishes we have served our friends over the past fifteen years. Some have come from friends and relatives, some have been inspired by dishes sampled at restaurants, and others have been invented—insofar as any dish can be "invented." For still other recipes, we started with ideas from classic cookbooks; like most people who spend a great deal of time in the kitchen, we have revised many such recipes over the years so that each has evolved, through many preparations, to reflect our own style of cooking. We have, naturally enough, drawn from those cuisines we most enjoy: Italian, French, Indian, Moroccan, Middle Eastern, and Eastern European. Although we appreciate Asian food, we felt the procedures and ingredients of that cuisine to be outside the scope and focus of this book.

There is something extraordinarily pleasing about having a soup or a stew simmering in the kitchen, with the myriad aromas scenting the rooms of the house on a dark winter afternoon. Certainly one of the great eating pleasures is to sit down in the dusk of a warm summer evening to a cold soup laced with fresh herbs. And one of the truly wonderful things about pasta is that it accommodates itself to any season, as well as to almost any ingredient. With as little as olive oil and garlic, or eggs and bacon, or a few vegetables, you can turn a pound of fettuccine into an extremely satisfying meal.

This volume is not meant as a "menu cookbook," and although it was our intention, in attempting to establish a balanced table of contents, that many of the dishes could go together, each dish has been chosen on its own merits. The "Accompaniments" section includes salads that can be served with many of the other recipes, a number of dishes that can be served as a first course or as part of an antipasto, and Indian condiments to go with the curries and tagines—or, for the adventurous, with the European stews.

We have tried to include not only classic recipes, such as Choucroute Garnie, Penne all'Arrabbiata, and Borscht, but also recipes that combine unusual ingredients, such as Portuguese Kale and Linguica Soup; Chicken Tagine with Prunes, Onions, and Almonds; and Spaghetti with Walnuts and Marjoram.

As you read through the recipes that follow, our tastes will become clear early on. We have a marked weakness for fresh coriander, garlic, cumin, dill, and anchovies. In fact, we both like highly spiced foods but have been careful to avoid extremes, striving for that miraculous golden mean. Although we believe each of these recipes can be followed exactly with outstanding results, every cook will undoubtedly want to add his or her own touch—a little more cayenne here, a little less garlic there, and so on. One can play with a soup, stew, or pasta—as one cannot with, say, a veal Prince Orloff or a cheese soufflé—without fear of total disaster.

These recipes have been written so that even a relative beginner in the kitchen can follow the directions. We do assume, however, that basic procedures have been mastered and that the reader has some familiarity with the vocabulary of cooking.

We do not argue for any particular school of cooking. This book simply reflects our personal taste, which, we believe, is eclectic. The sole criterion for inclusion in *The Good Food* is the proven excellence of a dish.

—Daniel Halpern and Julie Strand, 1985

ACKNOWLEDGMENTS

The authors would like to thank, first of all, Jeanne Halpern and Mark Strand, two people who played a critical part in the evolution of this book and shared directly our victories and temporary defeats. Thanks are also due to those good friends who participated at the experimental table, offering their considered opinions and suggestions: Bill and Sandy Bailey, William Davis, Harry and Kathleen Ford, Bob Hass, Moira Hodgson, Mike and Mary Keeley, Rosalind Krauss, Bill Matthews, Lani Poulson and Michael Ruddick, Tony and Elisabeth Sifton, Charlie and Helen Simic, Ray and Johanna Sokolov, Bill and Pat Strachan, and Charlie and Catherine Williams. We are also indebted to Jefferson Market, where most of the food in this book was purchased. Specifically: Dick Foody, Bill Kane, Al Landi, Mike Miller, Angelo Montuori, John Montuori, and "Cigar" Bill Ruocco.

And for instilling in us at an early age the satisfaction derived from preparing food for others, we are grateful to our mothers, Rosemary and Virginia.

We would also like to acknowledge our debt to the following writers, whose work we turned to again and again during the years that went into the preparation of this book: James Beard, Julia Child, Craig Claiborne, Michael Field, Roy Andries de Groot, Marcella Hazan, Julie Sahni, and Paula Wolfert.

Special thanks go to Lynne Fagles and Nancy Hanst, whose knowledge and advice—and generosity—helped make this book possible.

INGREDIENTS

It goes without saying that the better the ingredients, the better the dish. We believe that it is usually best to avoid the supermarket and buy your meat from a good butcher and your vegetables and fresh herbs from the greengrocer (if you can't grow your own). During some seasons fresh herbs may not be available; the recipes indicate when dried herbs may be substituted, but the difference is considerable, and if there is any way to find fresh herbs, do so. A few ingredients will have to be bought at specialty shops, which now exist in most cities throughout the country.

BEANS Dried beans, soaked overnight, are better in texture and flavor than canned beans. If you decide in the morning to prepare a dish that calls for beans that evening, here is an alternative method: In a large saucepan, cover 1 pound of beans with 2 quarts of water, bring to a boil, and cook for 4 or 5 minutes. Remove from the heat and let the beans soak in the hot water for 1 hour; then proceed as with soaked dried beans. If you decide on beans at the last minute, you may used canned beans, but the cooking time and amount of liquid must both be reduced.

BUTTER We always use unsalted butter—the taste is subtler and the bouquet while you're cooking is marvelous.

CILANTRO Also known as fresh coriander or Chinese parsley, cilantro is an extraordinary herb that has no substitute, so unique is its flavor. It figures heavily in the cuisines of Morocco, India, Mexico, and China. Under no circumstances buy the dried version. Following Julie Sahni's recommendations, we have found that cilantro can be stored for weeks in the refrigerator by wrapping a moist towel around the roots and then enclosing the towel and roots in a plastic bag, leaving the leaves free. For longer periods, purée the cilantro in a food processor with a quarter cup of water for each cup of tightly packed leaves, freeze in ice-cube trays, and transfer the cubes to a plastic freezer bag for storage (1 cube equals 2 tablespoons of fresh chopped leaves).

DRIED MUSHROOMS We have used only porcini in the recipes that call for dried mushrooms in this book. These are the Italian *Boletus edulis;* and their cousins, French or Polish cèpes, may be substituted. Asian varieties of dried mushrooms have a very different taste, not appropriate to these recipes.

LEMON JUICE Whenever lemon juice is called for, freshly squeezed lemon juice must be used. Do not substitute the bottled variety.

OLIVE OIL The best extra-virgin olive oil—green, fruity oil from the first pressing—is available in most good food stores; it is also quite expensive. However, it is our considered opinion that money spent on good olive oil is money well spent—it is used in many different recipes and its flavor is essential. Italian oil is apt to be fruity; the French is more refined; and the Spanish, although heavy, can also be good. Look for those oils with a green cast. Of the commercial oils, Bertolli and Progresso are acceptable if better oils are not available.

PARMESAN CHEESE Use only imported Italian Parmesan cheese. Buy it in a chunk and grate it yourself as needed. Carefully wrapped, a piece of Parmesan will keep for a couple of months in the refrigerator. Avoid prepackaged Parmesan at all costs.

PASTA We have included a recipe for fresh pasta on page 174, from which many types of pasta can be made. If you don't want to make your own pasta, and freshly made pasta is not readily available at a store near you, use boxed pasta, but only those brands imported from Italy. Three brands that seem consistently best and have the widest variety of shapes are De Cecco, Pastene, and Del Verde, but most Italian boxed pastas are good. For a recipe like Spaghetti alla Carbonara, boxed pasta may be preferable to fresh because it retains more heat and so achieves the final cooking of the sauce. The most important thing to remember is not to overcook pasta. It should always be cooked al dente, tender but firm to the bite.

SPICES AND DRIED HERBS Spices and dried herbs are generally better when bought loose and in small quantities, so buy them at a specialty shop if there's one near you. If not, we have found Spice Islands brand to be the best and freshest (although we prefer European bay leaves to the California laurel leaves they market).

TOMATOES Unless you have access to a vegetable garden, it is almost impossible to find tomatoes with acceptable texture and taste. If high-quality fresh tomatoes are not available, canned Italian tomatoes are a perfectly adequate substitute. After you have thoroughly drained a 35-ounce can of Italian plum tomatoes, run your thumb through each tomato to remove the seeds and excess liquid; you will then have about 1½ cups of tomato pulp. When a recipe calls for canned tomatoes, the measurement should be made *after* the tomatoes have been drained, seeded, and chopped. To peel fresh tomatoes, drop them into boiling water for 30 seconds, remove, and run under cold water to stop the cooking process. The skins can now be pulled off.

VINEGAR With vinegar, as with olive oil, you get what you pay for. Cheap vinegar tends to be raw, thin, and overly acidic. French and Italian vinegars are consistently the best. Use only wine vinegar, unless another type of vinegar is specified in the recipe.

WINE As we've already mentioned, the success of any dish depends on the quality of the individual ingredients that go into making it, and the same holds true for the wine you use in cooking. You should never use wine that you would not drink in a glass. For a few dollars you can buy quite serviceable red or white wines; it's also possible to find good Spanish sherry at a reasonable price— Tio Pepe is always a good bet. Stay away from anything labeled "Cooking Wine."

There are a number of good generic wines, red and white, from this country that are inexpensive and widely available.

When in doubt, a good wine store can lead you in the right direction.

SOUPS

Who has not experienced a sense of well-being upon sitting down to dinner at a friend's table to find already at each place a bowl of delicate and aromatic soup? To begin a meal with a soup course is to announce to the assembled guests that the hosts have taken the occasion seriously, that they have been attentive to the great tradition of dining. We have included a wide variety of first-course soups, ranging from the deceptively simple Double Consommé with Mushrooms to the spicy Cold Curried Tomato Soup with Mint to the complexly elegant Chestnut Soup with Brandy and Cream. Your choice of a first-course soup will, naturally, depend on your main course. We have tried to balance our offerings so that if your main dish happens to be the rich Lamb Stew with Eggplant, Saffron, and Ginger you have the option of selecting a soup that is on the light side, such as the delicate Coriander and Lemon Soup; or if you decide on the Veal Marengo, you might want to choose the Cream of Celery Root Soup, which has more body.

Some of the heartier soups—such as White Bean and Oxtail Soup or Red Snapper Chowder—make a perfect Sunday supper when accompanied by a salad, a loaf of French bread, and a bottle of good wine. These soups, if prepared over the weekend, make excellent quick meals during a busy week.

We have found that with any soup, using a homemade stock makes all the difference. This is particularly true when the stock itself is a major contributor to the flavor of the soup, as with Cold Avgolemono Soup or Escarole and Meatball Soup. As Michael Field wrote, "Although the preparation of a good stock is one of the least demanding culinary procedures, it does take time, which is doubtless why well-made soups appear so seldom on our tables." We have provided three basic stock recipes, which are surprisingly painless to make and will produce rich and flavorful stocks. You simply get them started and they cook themselves. Once made, chicken and beef stock will keep in the freezer almost indefinitely; fish stock fares less well and is best used right away. As far as we are concerned, there is no substitute for either homemade beef or fish stock, but if you do not have the time to make chicken stock from scratch, you can simmer a chopped onion, a carrot, a rib of celery, a few sprigs of parsley, a bay leaf, and a pinch of thyme in College Inn or Swanson's chicken broth for an hour and strain it.

You can purée most soups in a food processor, food mill, or blender, or with an immersion/stick blender. However, with a soup that is predominantly potato, only a food mill will do; a food processor creates an unpleasantly pasty quality.

It is important to keep in mind that, since most of our cream soups are thickened by the addition of egg yolks, aluminum pots (which we avoid in any case) must not be used—aluminum will both discolor and impart a metallic taste to the egg yolks. It is also important to keep a close eye on the final thickening process; if the soup is allowed to boil, the egg yolks will curdle.

CHICKEN STOCK

— MAKES 8-10 CUPS —

One 3–5 pound chicken, quartered

1 bay leaf

10 black peppercorns

10 sprigs parsley

4 celery stalks with leaves, quartered

2 carrots, peeled and quartered

2 medium leeks, with 1 inch of green, cleaned and sliced

2 medium onions, quartered

2 cloves garlic, crushed

3 quarts cold water (For an extra-rich stock that is basically a double consommé, we use College Inn or Swanson's chicken broth in place of water and eliminate the salt.)

2 teaspoons salt

¼ teaspoon dried thyme

1. In a large stockpot, combine all the ingredients except the thyme and bring to a boil, skimming the scum as it rises to the surface. Lower the heat, add the thyme, and simmer, partially covered, for 4 hours. It is important that the stock *not* boil; otherwise it will be cloudy.

2. Remove the bones and strain the stock through a fine sieve. Skim off as much fat as you can before using the stock; if possible, refrigerate the stock to allow the fat to solidify on the surface for easier removal.

BEEF STOCK

1 pound shin of beef, cut into
 2-inch chunks

3 pounds beef bones, split

2 veal knuckles

2 medium onions, quartered

2 carrots, peeled and
 quartered

2 celery stalks with leaves,
 quartered

2 leeks, with 1 inch of green,
 cleaned and sliced

1 turnip, peeled and sliced

2 cloves garlic, crushed

10 sprigs parsley

2 bay leaves

10 black peppercorns

2 teaspoons salt

1 cup dry white wine

4 quarts cold water

1. In a large stockpot, combine all the ingredients and bring to a boil, skimming off the scum as it rises to the surface. Lower the heat and simmer, partially covered, for at least 4 hours— preferably 5 or 6 hours. It is important that the stock not boil; otherwise it will be cloudy.

2. Remove the bones and strain the stock through a fine sieve. Skim off as much fat as you can before using the stock; if possible, refrigerate the stock to allow the fat to solidify on the surface for easier removal.

WHITE FISH STOCK

3 pounds fish trimmings (cod, tilefish, whiting, or any bony, nonoily fish)

1 clove garlic, crushed

1 medium onion, sliced

2 celery stalks with leaves, roughly chopped

2 leeks, with 1 inch of green, cleaned and sliced

1 carrot, peeled and chopped

2 sprigs fresh thyme (or ½ teaspoon dried thyme)

2 sprigs fresh tarragon (or ¼ teaspoon dried tarragon)

½ teaspoon fennel seeds, bruised

1 bay leaf

10 sprigs parsley

1 teaspoon salt

1 cup dry white wine

1. Wash the fish thoroughly—if fish heads are used, be sure to remove the gills. In a large stockpot, combine all the ingredients and 10 cups of water and bring to a boil, skimming the scum as it rises to the surface. Lower the heat and simmer, partially covered, for 40 minutes. Continue to skim every 5 minutes or so.

2. Strain the stock through a fine sieve. It is now ready to use. If possible, do not refrigerate or freeze fish stock; it's best to use it immediately, since it's never as good the next day.

DOUBLE CONSOMMÉ
WITH MUSHROOMS

This handsome-looking soup is a perfect beginning for a heavy meal. It is rich, yet delicate and elegant with the green garnish of scallions afloat in the steaming, teak-colored liquid. If this dish is to have its full effect, you must start with homemade chicken stock.

— SERVES 6 —

8 cups Chicken Stock (page 5)

One 3-pound chicken

5 sprigs parsley

1 carrot, peeled and quartered

1 celery stalk with leaves, quartered

1 medium onion stuck with a clove

1 clove garlic, crushed

1 bay leaf

1 ounce dried porcini mushrooms

1 cup hot water

2 pounds fresh mushrooms, trimmed

3 tablespoons butter

1 medium onion, chopped

½ cup dry white wine

1 tablespoon lemon juice

Salt and freshly ground pepper

Garnish: scallion greens, very thinly sliced

1. In a large saucepan, combine the stock, chicken, parsley, carrot, celery, onion stuck with a clove, garlic, and bay leaf and bring to a boil, skimming the scum as it rises to the surface. Lower the heat and simmer, partially covered, for 2 hours.

2. While the stock is cooking, in a small bowl cover the dried mushrooms with the hot water and let soak for at least 1 hour. Remove the mushrooms from the liquid, reserve, and strain the mushroom liquid through a sieve lined with several layers of cheesecloth. Reserve.

3. Chop the fresh mushrooms in a food processor in small batches, using a few short pulses so they are finely chopped but not liquefied. Set aside.

4. When the stock is finished strain it through a fine sieve into a bowl. Skim off as much surface fat as possible, or refrigerate and lift off the solidified fat. (The chicken will no longer be required, but it can be used to make chicken salad or our Fettuccine with Mushrooms, Chicken, and Cream, or it can just be eaten cold for a snack.)

5. In a large saucepan, heat the butter and the chopped onion, and cook over medium-low heat until soft. Add the chopped fresh mushrooms and continue cooking for another 10 minutes, stirring constantly. Add the stock, the reserved dried mushrooms and their liquid, the wine, lemon juice, and salt and pepper to taste. Simmer, partially covered, for 40 minutes.

6. Strain the soup through a fine sieve, pressing out as much liquid as possible, into a saucepan. Bring to just a boil, serve in heated bowls, and garnish with 4 or 5 slices of the scallion greens.

CORIANDER AND LEMON SOUP

This wonderfully light and subtle soup can be made only with fresh cilantro.

— SERVES 6 —

1 tablespoon coriander seeds

6 cups Chicken Stock (page 5)

1 leek, with 2 inches of green, cleaned and chopped

1 celery stalk, chopped

6 sprigs cilantro

¼ cup minced cilantro

1 tablespoon lemon juice

Salt and white pepper

Garnish: chopped cilantro

1. Toast the coriander seeds for 2 minutes in a heated skillet, without oil or butter, stirring constantly. Do not let the seeds burn; they should turn slightly golden.

2. In a large saucepan, combine the coriander seeds with the stock, leek, celery, and cilantro sprigs and bring to a boil. Lower the heat and simmer, covered, for 30 minutes.

3. Strain the soup into a saucepan, add the minced cilantro, lemon juice, and salt and pepper to taste, and simmer for another 5 minutes. Serve in heated bowls and garnish with the chopped cilantro.

COLD AVGOLEMONO SOUP

An egg and lemon soup that is to the Greeks what chicken soup is to the ailing.

— SERVES 6 —

6 cups Chicken Stock (page 5), fat completely removed

¼ cup long-grain rice, rinsed in cold water

1 teaspoon salt

3 eggs

¼ cup lemon juice

Garnish: chopped fresh chives or cilantro

1. In a large saucepan, bring the stock to a boil and add the rice and salt. Lower the heat and simmer, partially covered, until the rice is just barely done, about 15 minutes, and remove from the heat. Do not overcook the rice.

2. In a bowl, beat the eggs until they thicken and slowly beat in the lemon juice. Add a ladleful of the slightly cooled stock to the egg mixture and beat it for 30 seconds, then pour this mixture back into the stock, stirring constantly.

3. Heat the soup over low heat, stirring constantly, until it thickens. Be careful not to let the soup boil, or the eggs will curdle.

4. Pour the soup into a large bowl, and when it has cooled, refrigerate it, covered, for 3 or 4 hours, until it is cold. Serve in chilled bowls and garnish with the chopped fresh chives or cilantro.

JELLIED TOMATO AND ORANGE SOUP WITH DILL

1 small onion, chopped

1 clove garlic, crushed

½ teaspoon coriander seeds, bruised

½ teaspoon fennel seeds, bruised

2 sprigs parsley

2 cups dry white wine

¾ ounce (3 envelopes) powdered unflavored gelatin

2 cups tomato juice

2 cups freshly squeezed orange juice (from about 7 oranges), strained

2 cups Chicken Stock (page 5), fat completely removed

3 tablespoons chopped fresh dill

Salt and white pepper

Garnish: sour cream

1. In a small stainless steel saucepan, combine the onion, garlic, coriander seeds, fennel seeds, parsley, and white wine and bring to a boil over medium-high heat. Boil until the wine is reduced to 1 cup. Line a sieve with several layers of cheesecloth and set over a large bowl. Strain the liquid through the sieve. Add the gelatin and stir to dissolve it.

2. Stir in the tomato juice, orange juice, stock, dill, and salt and pepper to taste.

3. Cover the bowl and refrigerate, stirring occasionally to distribute the dill until the liquid sets, about 5 hours.

4. Break up the jellied soup into chunks and serve in chilled bowls. Garnish with the sour cream.

COLD CUCUMBER
AND YOGURT SOUP

A perfect soup for a summer night. Cool, attractive, and light enough to precede a stew, it is also quickly and easily made.

—— SERVES 6 ——

1 cup raisins

4 cups plain yogurt

1 cup light cream

1 cup milk

2 medium cucumbers, peeled, cut in half lengthwise, seeded, and diced

2 cloves garlic, minced

6 tablespoons minced fresh dill

Salt and white pepper

1 tablespoon cider vinegar

⅓ cup walnuts, roughly chopped

1. In a small bowl, soak the raisins in cold water to cover for 30 minutes. Drain.

2. In a large serving bowl, combine the yogurt, light cream, milk, cucumbers, garlic, dill, raisins, and salt and pepper to taste. Whisk in the vinegar and chill, covered, for at least 4 hours. Before serving, stir in the walnuts. Serve in chilled bowls.

VICHYSSOISE

The prototypical cold soup, vichyssoise is undoubtedly served at thousands of American tables over the course of a summer. But familiarity need not breed contempt—this cool, creamy blend of potato and leek is as satisfying now as it was in childhood, when it seemed a very sophisticated dish indeed. We sometimes garnish the soup with salmon roe instead of the traditional chives, or with a little of both. Do not, under any circumstances, be tempted to purée the base in a food processor—it is crucial that some texture remain in the soup.

— SERVES 8 —

4 tablespoons butter

6 leeks, white part only, cleaned and thinly sliced

3 large baking potatoes, peeled and cubed

1 bay leaf

6 cups Chicken Stock (page 5), fat completely removed

1 cup milk

1 cup heavy cream

Salt and white pepper

Garnish: chopped fresh chives or salmon roe or both

1. In a large saucepan, heat the butter over medium-low heat, add the leeks, and sauté until tender but not browned, about 10 minutes.

2. Add the potatoes, bay leaf, and stock and bring to a boil. Lower the heat and simmer, partially covered, until the potatoes are very tender, about 30 minutes.

3. Remove the bay leaf and purée the soup in a food mill or by rubbing it with a wooden spoon through a sieve into a large bowl.

4. Stir in the milk and cream and add salt and pepper to taste. Refrigerate, covered, for 3 or 4 hours, until thoroughly chilled.

5. Stir the soup before serving and taste again for salt and pepper. Serve in chilled bowls and garnish with the chopped fresh chives or salmon roe or both.

GAZPACHO ANDALUZ WITH CORNICHONS AND CREAM

There are endless versions of this traditional Spanish soup. Ours employs heavy cream and minced cornichons and is an ideal summer soup.

—— SERVES 8-10 ——

2 cups dry white wine

2 cloves garlic, chopped

1 teaspoon coriander seeds, bruised

½ teaspoon black peppercorns, bruised

1 bay leaf

7 cups tomato juice

4 ripe tomatoes, peeled, seeded, and chopped

1 large onion, chopped

3 medium cucumbers, peeled, cut in half lengthwise, seeded, and chopped

12 cornichons, chopped

Juice of 2 lemons

3 dashes Tabasco sauce

Salt and freshly ground pepper

1 cup heavy cream

Garnish: minced cornichons, chopped cilantro, and sliced scallions

1. In a large saucepan, combine the wine, garlic, coriander seeds, peppercorns, and bay leaf and cook over medium heat until the wine has reduced to 1 cup. Strain through a fine sieve into a bowl and reserve.

2. Combine 2 cups of the tomato juice, the tomatoes, onion, cucumbers, cornichons, lemon juice, and Tabasco sauce in a food processor and chop the vegetables, in short pulses, maintaining their texture and being careful not to liquefy them (this may be done in two batches).

3. Transfer to a bowl, stir in the remaining tomato juice, salt and pepper to taste, and reserved strained wine, and refrigerate, covered, for at least 24 hours—preferably 2 days.

4. Shortly before serving, whisk in the heavy cream, divide among chilled bowls, and garnish with the minced cornichons, chopped cilantro, and sliced scallions.

COLD BEET AND BUTTERMILK SOUP

—— SERVES 4-6 ——

8 medium beets (9 if you are using a beet for garnish)

3 tablespoons butter

1 small cucumber, peeled, cut in half lengthwise, seeded, and sliced

1 leek, with 1 inch of green, cleaned and chopped

2 cups Chicken Stock (page 5)

1 tomato, peeled, seeded, and chopped

Salt and freshly ground pepper

1 tablespoon lemon juice

¼ teaspoon freshly grated nutmeg

2 teaspoons prepared horseradish

2 tablespoons chopped fresh dill (or 2 teaspoons dried dill)

2 cups buttermilk

1 cup sour cream

Garnish: chopped fresh chives or julienned beet

1. In a saucepan, boil the beets in water to cover until they are tender, about 45 minutes. Drain and run under cold water. Remove the skins, chop the beets roughly, and set aside. (If you are using a beet for garnish, julienne it and set it aside at the same time.)

2. In a large saucepan, melt the butter, add the cucumber, leek, and beets, and cook over medium heat, stirring constantly, for 5 minutes.

3. Add the stock, tomato, and salt and pepper to taste and bring to a boil. Then reduce the heat and simmer, partially covered, for 30 minutes. Allow the mixture to cool slightly and purée it, in short pulses, in a food processor, or run it through a food mill. The mixture should retain some texture—that is, don't turn it into liquid.

4. Place the purée in a bowl and whisk in the lemon juice, nutmeg, horseradish, dill, buttermilk, and sour cream. Chill, covered, for at least 3 or 4 hours. Serve in chilled bowls and garnish with the chopped fresh chives or julienned beet.

COLD AVOCADO SOUP

An exceptionally simple and quick soup to make, this also happens to be velvety in texture and elegant in appearance, with notes of lemon and sherry behind the smooth taste of avocado.

—— SERVES 4-6 ——

2 ripe avocados, peeled, pitted, and quartered

2 cups Chicken Stock (page 5)

1 cup light cream

Juice of 2 lemons

1 clove garlic, minced

Salt and freshly ground pepper

2 tablespoons sherry

Garnish: chopped scallion greens

1. In a food processor, place the avocados, stock, cream, lemon juice, and garlic. Process until smooth.

2. Transfer to a large bowl and chill, covered, for 2 or 3 hours.

3. Add salt and pepper to taste. Stir in the sherry. Pour into chilled bowls and garnish with the chopped scallion greens.

COLD CURRIED TOMATO SOUP
WITH MINT

A very spicy soup, this is particularly refreshing on a hot day.

— SERVES 6 —

8 cups tomato juice

3 tablespoons tomato paste

2 tomatoes, peeled, seeded, and chopped

8 scallions, including some green, minced

2 teaspoons curry powder

¼ teaspoon ground cloves

½ teaspoon ground ginger

Juice and grated rind of 1 lemon

1 teaspoon sugar

1 teaspoon salt

1 cup sour cream

Garnish: chopped fresh mint

1. In a large bowl, combine all the ingredients except the salt and sour cream. Refrigerate, covered, for 3 hours or more.

2. Add salt to taste. Put the sour cream in a small bowl and thin it with about 1 cup of the tomato mixture, then whisk the diluted sour cream into the tomato mixture. Serve in chilled bowls and garnish with the chopped fresh mint.

COLD CURRIED ZUCCHINI SOUP

This was adapted from a recipe in Gourmet *magazine.*

— SERVES 4–6 —

6 tablespoons butter

1 small onion, minced

1 small leek, with 1 inch of green, cleaned and chopped

2 pounds zucchini, scrubbed, trimmed, and diced

1 tablespoon curry powder, or to taste

½ teaspoon ground cumin

2½ cups Chicken Stock (page 5)

2½ cups buttermilk

Salt and freshly ground pepper

Garnish: chopped cilantro or fresh parsley

1. In a large saucepan, melt the butter over medium-low heat, add the onion and leek, and sauté until tender. Lower the heat, add the zucchini, and cook, partially covered, until soft, about 10 minutes, stirring occasionally. Add the curry and cumin and cook, stirring constantly, for 3 minutes.

2. Remove the pan from the heat and stir in the chicken stock. Purée the mixture in a food processor or food mill, transfer to a large bowl, and stir in the buttermilk. Chill the soup for 3 or 4 hours.

3. Before serving, add salt and pepper to taste. Divide among chilled bowls and garnish with the chopped cilantro or fresh parsley.

COLD INDIAN ONION SOUP

This soup, based on a recipe by Miriam Ungerer,
may be served hot with equal success.

— SERVES 4 —

2 tablespoons butter

⅛ teaspoon saffron

1 tablespoon chopped fresh
thyme (or 1 teaspoon dried
thyme)

½ teaspoon ground coriander
seeds

1 teaspoon ground cumin

¼ teaspoon cayenne pepper

2 large onions, chopped

1 cup dry white wine

5 cups Beef Stock (page 6)

½ cup milk

Salt and freshly ground pepper

Garnish: chopped cilantro or
fresh parsley

1. In a large saucepan, melt the butter and mix in the saffron, thyme, ground coriander, cumin, and cayenne pepper. Cook the spices, stirring constantly, for 3 minutes, to release their flavors.

2. Add the onions and mix them into the spice mixture. Cover and cook over very low heat for 30 minutes.

3. Add the wine and cook for 5 minutes. Add the stock and bring the soup to a boil. Lower the heat and simmer, covered, for 30 minutes. Let the soup cool.

4. Purée the mixture in a food processor or food mill, transfer the purée to a bowl, and whisk in the milk. Refrigerate, covered, for 3 or 4 hours, or until completely chilled. Serve in chilled bowls and garnish with the chopped cilantro or fresh parsley.

COLD CURRIED PEA SOUP

— SERVES 6–8 —

4 tablespoons butter

2 medium onions, chopped

2 celery stalks with leaves, chopped

2 teaspoons curry powder

4 cups fresh peas (or frozen peas, defrosted)

1 large potato, peeled and finely diced

6 cups Chicken Stock (page 5)

1 bay leaf

1 cup chopped fresh parsley

1 cup heavy cream

Salt

Garnish: chopped fresh mint

1. In a large saucepan, heat the butter, add the onions and celery, and sauté over medium-low heat until soft. Add the curry powder and cook, stirring, for 1 minute.

2. Add the fresh peas and potato, enough of the stock to cover the vegetables, and the bay leaf. Bring to a boil, lower the heat, and simmer, partially covered, until the vegetables are tender, about 20 minutes. (If you are using frozen peas, add them after the potato has cooked for 15 minutes.)

3. Remove the bay leaf and stir in the parsley. Purée the mixture in a food processor or food mill.

4. Place the purée in a bowl and stir in the remaining stock. Cover and refrigerate for 3 or 4 hours, or until well chilled.

5. When ready to serve, stir in the heavy cream and salt to taste. Serve in chilled bowls and garnish with the chopped fresh mint.

MUSSEL BISQUE

3 pounds mussels

1 large onion, chopped

3 celery stalks with leaves, chopped

3 cloves garlic, 2 bruised and 1 minced

3 sprigs parsley

½ teaspoon dried thyme

½ teaspoon fennel seeds, bruised

1 bay leaf

Freshly ground pepper

2 cups dry white wine

4 tablespoons butter

3 leeks, white part only, cut in half lengthwise, cleaned, and thinly sliced

⅛ teaspoon freshly grated nutmeg

2 tablespoons lemon juice

Salt and white pepper

2 egg yolks

1 cup heavy cream

Garnish: chopped fresh parsley

1. Rinse the mussels under cold running water, rubbing the shells against each other to remove any encrustation. Remove the beards with a knife. Discard any mussels that seem unusually heavy.

2. In a large stockpot, place the onion, 1 of the celery stalks, the 2 bruised cloves of garlic, the parsley, thyme, fennel seeds, bay leaf, pepper, and wine. Bring to a boil, lower the heat, and simmer covered, for 15 minutes.

3. Raise the heat to high, and when the wine is boiling, add the mussels. Cover and cook, shaking the pot a couple of times, until the mussels open, about 5 minutes. Discard any mussels that have not opened.

4. Remove the mussels from the pot with tongs. Lift each mussel out of its shell, place in a bowl, and set aside. *Be sure there is no sand adhering to the mussels.*

5. Line a sieve with several layers of cheesecloth and set over a large measuring cup. Strain the cooking liquid through the sieve.

Add enough water or White Fish Stock (see page 7) to make 6 cups of liquid.

6. In a medium skillet, heat the butter over medium-low heat. Add the leeks and the remaining 2 chopped celery stalks and sauté until tender, about 20 minutes. Add the remaining minced garlic clove for the last minute of cooking.

7. Purée the vegetables with ½ cup of the diluted cooking liquid in a food processor or food mill. Put the purée in a mixing bowl and set aside.

8. In the food processor or food mill, purée the mussels in two batches, adding ½ cup of the diluted cooking liquid to each batch. With a wooden spoon, press the mussel purée through a sieve into the bowl of vegetable purée. Discard whatever will not pass through the sieve.

9. In a large saucepan, blend the purées and stir in the rest of the cooking liquid. Add the nutmeg and lemon juice and bring the soup to a simmer. Add salt and pepper to taste.

10. In a small bowl, beat the egg yolks into the heavy cream. Whisk in 1 ladleful of hot soup. Whisk this mixture into the soup, stirring constantly, and cook over low heat until the soup thickens. Do not allow the soup to boil or the eggs will curdle. Serve in heated bowls and garnish with the chopped fresh parsley.

CREAM OF ENDIVE SOUP

This is an unusual, rather refined, and slightly bitter soup, which should be considered only during endive season—winter through spring—to protect the budget.

— SERVES 6 —

4 tablespoons butter

6 medium Belgian endives, trimmed and chopped

3 scallions, white part only, sliced

1 small head Boston lettuce, chopped

1 teaspoon sugar

Salt and freshly ground pepper

4 cups Chicken Stock (page 5)

2 tablespoons lemon juice

1 cup milk

3 egg yolks

1 cup heavy cream

Garnish: chopped fresh dill

1. In a large saucepan, melt the butter. Add the endives, scallions, lettuce, sugar, and salt and pepper to taste and cook over medium heat, stirring, for about 5 minutes, until the vegetables soften.

2. Stir in the stock and lemon juice and bring to a boil. Lower the heat and simmer, partially covered, for 15 minutes.

3. Purée the mixture in a food processor or food mill and return it to the saucepan. Stir in the milk and bring the soup to a simmer.

4. In a bowl, beat the egg yolks into the heavy cream and then stir in 1 cup of the hot purée. Pour this mixture back into the purée and cook over low heat, stirring constantly, until the soup thickens, about 5 minutes. Do not allow the soup to boil or the eggs will curdle. Serve in heated bowls and garnish with the chopped fresh dill.

CREAM OF LETTUCE SOUP

— SERVES 6 —

3 tablespoons butter

1 medium onion, chopped

1 leek, with ½ inch of green, cleaned and chopped

1 medium head Boston lettuce, shredded

½ cup fresh peas (or frozen peas, defrosted)

4 cups Chicken Stock (page 5)

Salt and white pepper

2 egg yolks

1 cup heavy cream

Garnish: chopped fresh chervil or chives

1. In a large saucepan, melt the butter over medium heat, add the onion and leek, and cook until just soft. Add the lettuce, peas, and stock and bring to a boil. Lower the heat and simmer, covered, until the vegetables are tender, about 5 minutes.

2. Purée the mixture in a food processor or food mill until smooth. Return to the pan, bring to a boil, and remove from the heat. Add salt and pepper to taste.

3. In a small bowl, beat the egg yolks into the heavy cream and stir in 1 ladleful of the purée, whisking constantly. Whisk this mixture into the purée and whisk the soup over low heat until it thickens. Do not let the soup boil or the eggs will curdle. Serve in heated bowls and garnish with the chopped fresh chervil or chives.

CELERY, MUSHROOM, AND LETTUCE SOUP

We developed this soup with leftovers and some good rich chicken stock.
It's a simple and tasty soup, just right for lunch or a light dinner.

—— SERVES 4 ——

**1 ounce dried porcini
mushrooms**

1 cup hot water

3 tablespoons butter

1 small onion, chopped

3 celery stalks, chopped

**1 small head Boston lettuce,
shredded**

4 cups Chicken Stock (page 5)

3 egg yolks

½ cup buttermilk

1. In a small bowl, cover the dried mushrooms with the hot water and let soak for at least 1 hour. Remove the mushrooms from the liquid, chop, and set aside. Strain the liquid through a sieve lined with several layers of cheesecloth and reserve.

2. In a large saucepan, melt the butter over medium heat, add the onion and celery, and sauté until they soften a bit. Add the lettuce and continue cooking until it wilts, about 3 minutes. Add the stock, the mushrooms, and the reserved mushroom liquid and bring to a boil. Lower the heat and simmer, partially covered, for 30 minutes.

3. After the mixture cools a bit, purée it in a food processor or food mill until smooth and return it to the saucepan.

4. In a small bowl, beat the egg yolks into the buttermilk and whisk in 1 ladleful of the hot soup. Slowly whisk this mixture into the soup and cook slowly and carefully until the soup thickens. Do not allow the soup to boil or the eggs will curdle. Serve in heated bowls.

CREAM OF CUCUMBER SOUP

— SERVES 4 —

3 tablespoons butter

1 medium onion, chopped

4 cucumbers, peeled, cut lengthwise, seeded, and roughly chopped

½ head Boston lettuce, chopped

3 cups Chicken Stock (page 5)

2 cups buttermilk

1 tablespoon chopped fresh dill (or 1 teaspoon dried dill)

¼ teaspoon freshly grated nutmeg

¼ cup dry white wine

3 egg yolks

½ cup heavy cream

Garnish: thinly sliced cucumber or chopped fresh parsley

1. In a large saucepan, heat the butter, add the onion, and sauté until soft. Add the cucumbers and lettuce, stir, and cook for 2 minutes.

2. Add the stock and bring to a boil. Lower the heat and simmer, partially covered, for 30 minutes.

3. Purée the mixture in a food processor or food mill and return to the saucepan. Add the buttermilk, dill, nutmeg, and wine and simmer for 5 minutes.

4. In a small bowl, beat the egg yolks into the heavy cream and whisk in 1 ladleful of the purée. Whisk this mixture into the soup and heat slowly and carefully, stirring constantly, over low heat until the soup thickens. Do not let the soup boil or the eggs will curdle. Serve in heated bowls, and garnish with the thinly sliced cucumber or chopped fresh parsley.

CREAM OF ASPARAGUS SOUP

— SERVES 8 —

1½ pounds asparagus

4 tablespoons butter

2 leeks, with 1 inch of green, cleaned, cut in half, and sliced

2 cloves garlic, minced

1 large potato, peeled and diced

7 cups Chicken Stock (page 5)

½ teaspoon salt

3 egg yolks

1 cup heavy cream

Salt and white pepper

3 tablespoons lemon juice

1. Remove the tips from the asparagus and set aside. Snap off the tough bottoms from the stalks and discard. Cut the stalks into 1-inch lengths and set aside.

2. In a large saucepan, heat the butter, add the leeks, and sauté over medium-low heat until tender. Add the garlic for the last minute of cooking.

3. Add the asparagus stalks, potato, and enough stock to cover the vegetables and bring to a boil. Lower the heat and simmer, partially covered, until the vegetables are tender, about 30 minutes.

4. While the vegetables are cooking, bring 2 cups of water and the ½ teaspoon of salt to a boil in a small saucepan. Add the asparagus tips and cook until just tender, about 5 minutes. Drain and set aside on paper towels.

5. When the vegetables in the stock are tender, purée the mixture in a food processor or food mill.

6. Return the purée to the saucepan. Add the remaining stock, bring to a simmer, and remove from the heat.

7. In a small bowl, beat the egg yolks into the heavy cream and whisk in 1 ladleful of the hot soup. Whisk this mixture into the hot soup and cook over low heat, stirring constantly, until the soup thickens. Do not allow the soup to boil or the eggs will curdle. Add salt and pepper to taste.

8. When the soup has thickened, stir in the lemon juice and the asparagus tips. Serve in heated bowls.

CREAM OF CELERY AND TOMATO SOUP

4 tablespoons butter

10 celery stalks with leaves, chopped

1 medium onion, chopped

1 teaspoon sweet Hungarian paprika

6 cups Chicken Stock (page 5)

1 bay leaf

½ teaspoon dried summer savory

3 tomatoes, peeled, seeded, and chopped

Salt and white pepper

½ cup heavy cream

½ cup sour cream, at room temperature

3 egg yolks

Garnish: chopped fresh parsley

1. In a large saucepan, melt the butter, add the celery and onion, and cook over medium-low heat, stirring, for 15 minutes. For the last minute of cooking, add the paprika and stir. Add half the stock, or enough to cover the vegetables, the bay leaf, and the savory and bring to a boil. Lower the heat and simmer, partially covered, for 20 minutes, or until the vegetables are tender.

2. Remove the bay leaf and purée the vegetables in a food processor or food mill.

3. Put the purée in a stainless steel saucepan and add the remaining stock and the tomatoes. Bring to a boil, lower the heat, and simmer for 5 minutes. Add salt and pepper to taste.

4. In a small bowl, blend the heavy cream and sour cream and beat in the egg yolks. Whisk in 1 ladleful of the hot soup. Whisk this mixture into the soup and simmer until it thickens, stirring constantly. Do not allow the soup to boil or the eggs will curdle. Serve in heated bowls and garnish with the chopped fresh parsley.

CREAM OF CELERY ROOT SOUP

5 tablespoons butter

1 large onion, chopped

1 large potato, peeled and cubed

3 celery roots, peeled and cubed

1 bay leaf

8 cups Chicken Stock (page 5)

1½ teaspoons chopped fresh tarragon (or ½ teaspoon dried tarragon)

Salt and white pepper

½ cup sour cream, at room temperature

½ cup heavy cream

3 egg yolks

Garnish: chopped celery leaves

1. In a large saucepan, melt 4 tablespoons of the butter over medium-low heat, add the onion, and sauté until soft.

2. Add the potato, celery roots, bay leaf, and enough stock to cover the vegetables and bring to a boil. Lower the heat and simmer, partially covered, until the vegetables are tender, about 20 minutes.

3. Remove the bay leaf and purée the vegetables in a food processor or food mill.

4. Return the purée to the pan. Add the remaining stock and tarragon, bring to a simmer, season with salt and pepper to taste.

5. In a small bowl, blend the sour cream and heavy cream and beat in the egg yolks. Whisk in 1 ladleful of hot soup and whisk this mixture into the soup, stirring constantly. Cook until the soup is heated through. Do not allow the soup to boil or the eggs will curdle.

6. Remove from the heat and stir in the remaining tablespoon of butter, softened. Serve in heated bowls and garnish with the chopped celery leaves.

SPINACH SOUP WITH PARMESAN CHEESE

2 pounds fresh spinach, or
2 10-ounce boxes frozen
chopped spinach, defrosted

4 tablespoons butter

1 large onion, chopped

2 cloves garlic, minced

8 cups Chicken Stock
(page 5)

¼ teaspoon freshly grated
nutmeg

2 tablespoons chopped
fresh basil (or 1 teaspoon
dried basil)

1 cup heavy cream

½ cup freshly grated
Parmesan

Salt and white pepper

Garnish: Croutons (recipe
follows)

1. If you are using fresh spinach, wash it carefully and remove the thick stems. In a stainless steel stockpot, cook the spinach over low heat in only the water that clings to the leaves, stirring it until it wilts. Chop and set aside. If you are using frozen spinach, defrost entirely and squeeze lightly to extract excess liquid.

2. In a large saucepan, heat the butter over low heat, add the onion, and sauté until is soft. Add the garlic for the last minute of cooking. (*Note:* If using dried basil, add it with the garlic.)

3. Add 4 cups of the stock, the spinach, and nutmeg and bring to a boil. Lower the heat and simmer, partially covered, for 10 minutes.

4. Purée the mixture with the fresh basil in a food processor or food mill and return the purée to the saucepan. Add the remaining 4 cups of stock and the heavy cream. Bring the soup to a simmer, stirring occasionally. When the soup is hot, remove it from the heat and stir in the Parmesan. Add salt and pepper to taste. Serve in heated bowls and garnish with the croutons.

CROUTONS

8 slices stale Italian or French bread
½ cup olive oil

1. Remove the crusts from the bread and cut the bread into ½-inch cubes.

2. In a skillet, heat half the oil over medium-high heat, add half the bread cubes, and fry them, stirring constantly, until browned on all sides. Drain on paper towels. Repeat for the remaining bread cubes. Set aside until ready to use.

SORREL SOUP

This creamy, slightly sour soup is dominated by the distinctive, lemony taste of its green, and we think it's a mistake to complicate it with even so much as a touch of nutmeg or a garnish of mimosa. It may be served hot or cold. If you serve it cold, make it in the morning and chill it for at least 4 hours.

—— SERVES 8 ——

4 tablespoons butter

3 leeks, cut in half lengthwise, cleaned and white part finely sliced

2 cloves garlic, minced

2 pounds sorrel, washed and roughly chopped

6 cups Chicken Stock (page 5)

1 cup chopped fresh parsley

Salt and white pepper

3 egg yolks

1 cup heavy cream

1. In a large stainless steel saucepan, heat the butter over medium-low heat, add the leeks, and sauté until tender. Add the garlic for the last minute of cooking.

2. Add the sorrel, toss it with the leeks and butter, cover, and continue cooking, turning the sorrel a few times with a wooden spoon, until it wilts, about 5 minutes. Add 4 cups of the stock and simmer, uncovered, for 15 minutes. Stir in the parsley.

3. Purée the mixture in a food mill or food processor and return the purée to the saucepan. Add the remaining 2 cups of stock, bring to a simmer, and add salt and pepper to taste.

4. In a small bowl, beat the egg yolks into the heavy cream and whisk in a ladleful of hot soup. Whisk this mixture into the soup and heat, stirring constantly, until the soup thickens. Do not allow the soup to boil or the eggs will curdle.

5. Serve in heated bowls.

MUSHROOM SOUP

2 ounces dried porcini
mushrooms

1 cup port, heated in a
saucepan

3 tablespoons butter

6 scallions, white part only,
sliced

1 pound fresh mushrooms,
chopped

3 tablespoons flour

5 cups Chicken Stock (page 5)

1 tablespoon lemon juice

3 dashes Tabasco

Salt and freshly ground pepper

1 cup sour cream, at room
temperature

Garnish: chopped fresh
parsley

1. In a small bowl, cover the dried mushrooms with the port and let them soak for at least 1 hour. Remove the mushrooms from the liquid, chop, and set aside. Strain the liquid through a sieve lined with several layers of cheesecloth and reserve.

2. In a large saucepan, heat the butter over medium heat. Add the scallions and sauté until barely soft. Add the fresh mushrooms and sauté for another 10 minutes, stirring frequently. Sprinkle the mushrooms with the flour and cook for 3 minutes, continuing to stir.

3. Add the stock and the chopped dried mushrooms and their liquid, and bring the mixture to a boil. Lower the heat and simmer, covered, for 1 hour.

4. Purée the mixture in a food mill or food processor and return to the saucepan, adding the lemon juice. Add salt and pepper to taste. Bring to a boil and remove from the heat. In a small bowl, whisk a ladleful of the hot soup into the sour cream and whisk this mixture into the soup. Serve in heated bowls and garnish with the chopped fresh parsley.

CREAM OF CARROT SOUP

— SERVES 8 —

4 tablespoons butter

2 leeks, white part only, cleaned and thinly sliced

1 medium onion, chopped

10 carrots, peeled and sliced

2 large potatoes, peeled and cubed

1 bay leaf

8 cups Chicken Stock (page 5)

¼ cup lemon juice

¼ teaspoon freshly grated nutmeg

Salt and white pepper

3 egg yolks

1 cup heavy cream

Garnish: chopped fresh chives or parsley

1. In a large saucepan, heat the butter. Add the leeks and onion and cook over medium-low heat until tender.

2. Add the carrots, potatoes, bay leaf, and enough stock to cover the vegetables and bring to a boil. Lower the heat and simmer, covered, until the vegetables are tender, about 30 minutes.

3. Remove the bay leaf, purée the mixture in a food mill, and return the purée to the saucepan. Add the remaining stock, the lemon juice, and nutmeg. Bring to a simmer and add salt and pepper to taste.

4. In a small bowl, beat the egg yolks into the heavy cream and whisk in a ladleful of hot soup. Whisk this mixture into the soup and cook, stirring constantly, until it thickens. Do not allow the soup to boil or the eggs will curdle. Serve in heated bowls and garnish with the chopped fresh chives or parsley.

CREAM OF LIMA BEAN SOUP WITH MARJORAM

3 tablespoons butter

1 medium onion, chopped

2 cloves garlic, minced

Three 10-ounce packages frozen baby lima beans, defrosted

¾ teaspoon dried marjoram

7 cups Chicken Stock (page 5)

½ cup chopped fresh parsley

Salt and white pepper

1 cup heavy cream

Garnish: 1 large tomato, peeled, seeded, and chopped

1. In a large saucepan, melt the butter, add the onion, and cook over medium-low heat until soft. Add the garlic for the last minute of cooking.

2. Add the lima beans, marjoram, and enough stock to cover them, and bring to a boil. Lower the heat and simmer, partially covered, until the beans are soft, about 20 minutes. Stir in the parsley.

3. Purée the mixture in a food processor or food mill and return to the saucepan. Add the remaining stock and bring to a simmer. Add salt and pepper to taste.

4. Stir in the heavy cream and heat. Serve in heated bowls and garnish with the chopped tomato.

CREAM OF BROCCOLI SOUP

2 tablespoons butter

1 small onion, finely chopped

2 cloves garlic, minced

1 medium potato, peeled and cubed

7 cups Chicken Stock (page 5)

1 bay leaf

½ teaspoon salt

1 head broccoli, cut into small florets, the stalk cut into ¼-inch slices

1 tablespoon lemon juice

¼ teaspoon freshly grated nutmeg

3 egg yolks

1 cup sour cream, at room temperature

Salt and white pepper

Garnish: minced scallion greens

1. In a large saucepan, melt the butter, add the onion, and cook over medium-low heat until soft but not brown. Add the garlic for the last minute of cooking.

2. Add the potato, 5 cups of the stock, the bay leaf, and salt. Bring to a boil, lower the heat, and simmer, partially covered, until the potato is just tender, about 10 minutes.

3. Add the broccoli and cook until just tender, about 5 minutes.

4. Remove the bay leaf and purée the mixture in a food processor or food mill. Return to the saucepan and add the remaining stock, lemon juice, and nutmeg. Bring the soup to a simmer.

5. In a small bowl, beat the egg yolks into the sour cream and whisk in a ladleful of hot soup. Whisk this mixture into the hot soup, stirring constantly, and cook over low heat until the soup thickens. Do not allow the soup to boil or the eggs will curdle. Add salt and pepper to taste. Serve in heated bowls and garnish with the minced scallion greens.

CREAM OF CAULIFLOWER SOUP

— SERVES 4 —

3 tablespoons butter

1 head cauliflower, chopped, with leaves and tough part of stem removed

4 leeks, white part only, cleaned and sliced

2 cups Chicken Stock (page 5)

2 cups milk

½ cup ricotta cheese

¼ teaspoon freshly grated nutmeg

Salt and white pepper

4 tablespoons freshly grated Parmesan

3 egg yolks

1 cup heavy cream

2 tablespoons softened butter

Garnish: chopped fresh parsley

1. In a large saucepan, heat the butter, add the cauliflower and leeks, and cook over medium-low heat for 5 minutes, stirring constantly.

2. Add the stock, bring to a boil, lower the heat, and simmer, covered, for 25 minutes.

3. Purée the vegetables in a food mill or food processor and return to the saucepan. Whisk in the milk, ricotta cheese, nutmeg, salt and white pepper to taste, and Parmesan and bring to a simmer, stirring constantly. Remove from the heat.

4. In a small bowl, beat the egg yolks into the heavy cream. Whisk in 1 ladleful of the soup. Whisk this mixture into the soup and heat over low heat, stirring, until the soup thickens. Do not allow the soup to boil or the eggs will curdle. Remove from the heat and stir in the softened butter. Serve in heated bowls and garnish with the chopped fresh parsley.

ARTICHOKE SOUP

— SERVES 4 —

5 large artichokes, washed
and trimmed

3 tablespoons butter

1 medium onion, chopped

2 cloves garlic, chopped

4 cups Chicken Stock (page 5)

¼ cup dry white wine

1 teaspoon chopped fresh mint
(or ⅓ teaspoon dried mint)

3 egg yolks

½ cup heavy cream

Salt and freshly ground pepper

Garnish: chopped fresh mint

1. In a saucepan, place the artichokes with water to cover and bring to a boil. Cover and cook until they are very tender, about 45 minutes, depending on the size of the artichokes. Remove from the heat, drain, and allow the artichokes to cool, tips down.

2. In a large saucepan, heat the butter, add the onion, and sauté over medium-low heat until soft. Add the garlic for the last minute of cooking. Stir in 1 cup of the stock, the wine, and mint and bring to a boil. Lower the heat and simmer, covered, for 5 minutes. Remove from the heat.

3. When the artichokes are cool enough to handle, scrape the insides of the leaves into a food processor. This may take a little time, but there is a surprising amount of meat on the leaves. After this has been completed, remove the artichoke hearts and add them to the processor. Add the wine/stock mixture and purée the ingredients until smooth. Return the mixture to the saucepan with the remaining stock. Bring to a simmer and remove from the heat.

4. In a small bowl, beat the egg yolks into the heavy cream and whisk in 1 ladleful of the hot soup. Whisk this mixture into the soup, add salt and pepper to taste, and heat slowly and carefully, stirring constantly, until the soup thickens. Do not let the soup boil or the eggs will curdle. Serve in heated bowls and garnish with the chopped fresh mint.

CREAM OF BRUSSELS SPROUTS SOUP

4 tablespoons butter

1 large onion, chopped

2 celery stalks with leaves, chopped

2 medium potatoes, peeled and diced

6 cups Brussels sprouts, trimmed and quartered

7 cups Chicken Stock (page 5)

¼ teaspoon freshly grated nutmeg

Salt and white pepper

3 egg yolks

1 cup heavy cream

Garnish: chopped fresh parsley

1. In a saucepan, heat the butter over medium-low heat, add the onion and celery, and sauté until tender but not browned.

2. Add the potatoes, Brussels sprouts, and enough stock to cover the vegetables and bring to a boil. Lower the heat and simmer, covered, until the vegetables are tender, about 30 minutes.

3. Purée the vegetables in a food mill or food processor and return the purée to the pan. Add the remaining stock and the nutmeg. Bring to a simmer and add salt and pepper to taste.

4. In a small bowl, beat the egg yolks into the heavy cream and whisk in 1 ladleful of the hot soup. Whisk this mixture into the soup and, heat, stirring, until the soup thickens. Do not allow the soup to boil or the eggs will curdle. Serve in heated bowls and garnish with the chopped fresh parsley.

BUTTERNUT SQUASH SOUP

—— SERVES 4-6 ——

3 tablespoons butter

2 small butternut squash, peeled, seeded, and chopped

2 leeks, white part only, cleaned and chopped

1 medium potato, peeled and chopped

3 green cooking apples, peeled, cored, and chopped

3 scallions, with 1 inch of green, chopped

3 shallots, chopped

1 tablespoon chopped fresh tarragon (or ½ teaspoon dried tarragon)

1 tablespoon chopped fresh basil (or ½ teaspoon dried basil)

4 cups Chicken Stock (page 5)

1 cup dry white wine

Salt and freshly ground pepper

½ cup light cream

Garnish: chopped fresh chives

1. In a large saucepan, heat the butter, add the squash, leeks, potato, apples, scallions, shallots, tarragon, and basil, and sauté over medium heat, stirring constantly, for 5 minutes.

2. Add the stock, wine, and salt and pepper to taste and bring to a boil. Lower the heat and simmer, covered, until the vegetables are tender, about 45 minutes.

3. Purée the mixture in a food processor or food mill and return to the saucepan. Mix in the light cream and bring just to a simmer. Serve in heated bowls and garnish with the chopped fresh chives.

CHESTNUT SOUP WITH BRANDY AND CREAM

1½ pounds fresh chestnuts
(or two 15½-ounce cans
prepared chestnuts)

1 tablespoon vegetable oil

BOUQUET GARNI

1 carrot, peeled and quartered

1 celery stalk with leaves,
quartered

10 sprigs parsley

¼ teaspoon dried thyme

1 medium onion stuck with
2 cloves

5 cups Chicken Stock (page 5)

¼ teaspoon freshly grated
nutmeg

½ cup heavy cream

3 tablespoons brandy

Salt and freshly ground pepper

Garnish: chopped fresh parsley

1. If you are using fresh chestnuts, preheat the oven to its highest setting (not broil). Line a flat pan with foil and coat it lightly with the oil. Make an X with a sharp knife on the round side of each chestnut and place them on the pan. Roast the chestnuts for 15 minutes, shaking the pan once or twice during the cooking. Take the chestnuts out of the oven, and peel off the shells and skins while they are still warm.

2. In a large saucepan, combine the chestnuts, the bouquet garni, the onion, and the stock. Bring to a boil, then lower the heat and simmer, covered, for 45 minutes (15 minutes if you are using canned chestnuts), or until the chestnuts are tender.

3. Remove the bouquet garni and discard. Purée the mixture in a food mill or food processor and return it to the pan. Whisk in the nutmeg, heavy cream, brandy, and salt and pepper to taste and bring to a simmer. Serve in heated bowls and garnish with the chopped fresh parsley.

JERUSALEM ARTICHOKE SOUP

— SERVES 8 —

2 pounds Jerusalem artichokes

Juice of 1 lemon

4 tablespoons butter

2 medium onions, chopped

1 celery stalk with leaves, chopped

2 cloves garlic, minced

8 cups Chicken Stock (page 5)

1 bay leaf

Salt and white pepper

3 egg yolks

½ cup heavy cream

Garnish: chopped fresh summer savory or parsley

1. Wash and peel the artichokes, cube them, and drop them into a bowl of water with the lemon juice added.

2. Drain the artichokes. In a large heavy pot, melt the butter, add the artichokes, onions, and celery, and cook over medium-low heat, until they begin to soften but have not colored. Add the garlic for the last minute of cooking.

3. Add enough stock to cover the vegetables, bay leaf, and salt to taste and bring to a boil. Lower the heat and simmer, partially covered, until the vegetables are soft, about 20 minutes.

4. Remove the bay leaf. Purée the vegetables in a food processor or food mill and return to the saucepan. Add the remaining stock and bring to a simmer. Add salt and pepper to taste.

5. In a small bowl, beat the egg yolks into the heavy cream and whisk in 1 ladleful of the hot soup. Whisk this mixture into the soup and cook over low heat, stirring constantly, until the soup thickens. Do not allow the soup to boil or the eggs will curdle. Serve in heated bowls and garnish with the chopped fresh summer savory or parsley.

TURNIP, POTATO, AND LEEK SOUP

— SERVES 8 —

5 tablespoons butter

3 leeks, white part only, cleaned and sliced

1 celery stalk with leaves, chopped

1 small onion, chopped

6 cups Chicken Stock (page 5)

3 large potatoes, peeled and cubed

4 medium turnips, peeled and cubed

Salt and white pepper

3 egg yolks

1 cup heavy cream

Garnish: chopped fresh summer savory or parsley

1. In a heavy saucepan, heat 4 tablespoons of the butter, add the leeks, celery, and onion, and sauté over low heat until soft.

2. Add the stock, potatoes, and turnips and bring to a boil. Lower the heat and simmer, partially covered, until the vegetables are soft, about 40 minutes.

3. Purée the mixture in a food mill and return to the saucepan. Heat the purée over medium heat and add salt and pepper to taste.

4. In a small bowl, beat the egg yolks into the heavy cream and whisk in 1 ladleful of the hot purée. Whisk this mixture into the purée and cook over low heat, stirring constantly, until the soup thickens. Do not allow the soup to boil or the eggs will curdle.

5. Remove from the heat and stir in the remaining tablespoon of butter. Serve in heated bowls and garnish with the chopped fresh summer savory or parsley.

ALSATIAN POTATO AND ONION SOUP

This soup uses as a base a very hearty stock made with veal, beef, and chicken. The finished soup has sweetish highlights that derive from the intermingling of the onions, tarragon, Riesling wine, and Appenzeller cheese. It is based on a soup sampled at Sam Hayward's restaurant, 22 Lincoln, in Brunswick, Maine.

—— SERVES 8 ——

STOCK

8 cups Chicken Stock (page 5)

5 chicken wings

1 pound shin of beef

2 veal knuckles

2 pounds beef bones

10 sprigs parsley

2 cloves garlic, crushed

1 bay leaf

2 carrots, peeled and sliced

2 large onions, chopped

2 celery stalks, chopped

10 peppercorns

2 tablespoons peanut oil

2 medium onions, thinly sliced

2 tablespoons chopped fresh basil (or 2 teaspoons dried basil)

1 tablespoon chopped fresh tarragon (or 1 teaspoon dried tarragon)

1 tablespoon chopped fresh thyme (or 1 teaspoon dried thyme)

1 clove garlic, minced

1½ cups Riesling or Gewürtztraminer (it is imperative that the wine be slightly sweet)

1½ pounds potatoes, peeled and very finely diced

Salt and freshly ground pepper

¼ pound Appenzeller or Gruyère cheese, very finely diced

¾ cup heavy cream

Garnish: chopped fresh tarragon or chives

1. In a stockpot, combine the stock ingredients and bring to a boil, skimming off the scum as it rises to the surface. Simmer, partially covered, for 3 hours. Strain and let cool—or refrigerate overnight, if possible. Skim off the fat on the surface.

2. In a large saucepan, heat the peanut oil over medium-high heat, add the sliced onions, and sauté until they are uniformly golden. Add the basil, tarragon, thyme, and minced garlic for the last minute of cooking.

3. Add the wine and simmer for 3 minutes. Stir in the stock and bring to a slow boil.

4. Add the potatoes and cook until they crumble easily, about 45 minutes. With a wire whisk, crush some of the potatoes and blend them with the stock. Adjust the seasoning with salt and pepper to taste. Stir in the cheese and remove from the heat. Swirl in the cream. Serve in heated bowls and garnish with a sprinkling of the chopped fresh tarragon or chives.

POTATO AND ESCAROLE SOUP

— SERVES 8 —

4 tablespoons butter

2 medium onions, chopped

1 celery stalk with leaves, chopped

3 cloves garlic, minced

3 large potatoes, peeled and cubed

8 cups Chicken Stock (page 5)

1 bay leaf

Salt and white pepper

1 head escarole (about 1 pound), shredded

1 cup heavy cream

¼ teaspoon freshly grated nutmeg

Garnish: grated lemon rind and chopped fresh parsley

1. In a large saucepan, heat the butter, add the onions and celery, and sauté over medium-low heat until tender. Add the garlic for the last minute of cooking.

2. Add the potatoes, enough stock to cover the vegetables, and the bay leaf and bring to a boil. Lower the heat and simmer, partially covered, until the potatoes are very soft, about 30 minutes.

3. Remove the bay leaf. Purée the vegetables in a food mill and return to the saucepan. Add the remaining stock, bring to a simmer, and add salt and pepper to taste.

4. Add the escarole and simmer, uncovered, until it is tender, about 10 minutes. Stir in the cream and nutmeg and bring to a simmer. Serve in heated bowls and garnish with the grated lemon rind and chopped fresh parsley.

CURRIED EGGPLANT SOUP

This sturdy winter soup, passed on to us in a slightly different form by Ann Laughlin, is wonderfully scented with curry and rosemary.

— SERVES 4 —

¼ cup olive oil

1 medium eggplant, peeled and cubed

2 tablespoons butter

1 small onion, chopped

2 cloves garlic, chopped

1 teaspoon curry powder

2 tablespoons flour

1 cup milk

3 cups Chicken Stock (page 5)

¼ teaspoon rosemary, crushed

Salt and freshly ground pepper

Garnish: chopped fresh parsley or cilantro

1. In a heavy skillet, heat the oil, add the eggplant, and cook over medium heat until it turns light brown, about 15 minutes. Set aside on paper towels to drain.

2. In a large saucepan, heat the butter, add the onion and garlic, and cook over medium heat until just soft.

3. In a small bowl, combine the curry powder and flour, stir it into the onion/garlic mixture until thoroughly blended, and continue to cook for 3 minutes. Add the milk, a little at a time, stirring constantly until the mixture thickens slightly.

4. Add the stock, rosemary, and eggplant and simmer for 15 minutes. Remove from the heat and cool slightly.

5. Purée the mixture in a food processor or food mill and return it to the saucepan. Add salt and pepper to taste and bring to a boil. Serve in heated bowls and garnish with the chopped fresh parsley or cilantro.

CURRIED CREAM OF PARSNIP SOUP

— SERVES 8 —

3 tablespoons butter

1 large onion, chopped

1 tablespoon curry powder

1 large potato, peeled and cubed

6 large parsnips, peeled and cubed

1 bay leaf

7 cups Chicken Stock (page 5)

½ cup freshly squeezed orange juice

3 egg yolks

1 cup heavy cream

Salt and white pepper

Garnish: chopped cilantro or fresh parsley

1. In a large saucepan, heat the butter, add the onion, and sauté over medium-low heat for 5 minutes. Add the curry powder, stir, and cook until the onion is soft.

2. Add the potato, parsnips, bay leaf, and enough stock to cover the vegetables and bring to a boil. Lower the heat and simmer, partially covered, until the vegetables are tender, about 20 minutes.

3. Remove the bay leaf. Purée the mixture in a food processor or food mill and return the purée to the saucepan. Add the remaining stock and the orange juice, bring to a simmer, and remove from heat.

4. In a small bowl, beat the egg yolks into the heavy cream. Whisk in 1 ladleful of hot soup. Whisk this mixture into the soup and heat over low heat, stirring constantly, until it thickens. Do not allow the soup to boil or the eggs will curdle. Add salt and pepper to taste. Serve in heated bowls and garnish with the chopped cilantro or fresh parsley.

MULLIGATAWNY

There are many different ways to make this classic Indian soup.
The version that follows is a variation on a Julie Sahni recipe.

—— SERVES 4 ——

4 cups Chicken Stock (page 5)

1 potato, peeled and chopped

1 carrot, peeled and chopped

1 medium onion, roughly
  chopped

1 celery stalk, chopped

¼ pound fresh mushrooms

3 sprigs parsley

3 tablespoons butter

1 medium onion, minced

1 teaspoon minced fresh
  ginger

2 cloves garlic, minced

2 tablespoons flour

½ teaspoon ground cumin

½ teaspoon ground coriander

¼ teaspoon turmeric

Salt and freshly ground pepper

½ cup plain yogurt

1. In a large saucepan, combine the stock, potato, carrot, chopped onion, celery, mushrooms, and parsley, bring to a boil, and then reduce to a simmer for 30 minutes. Purée the mixture in a food processor or food mill and rub through a sieve back into the saucepan.

2. In a skillet, heat the butter, add the minced onion, and cook, stirring constantly, until the mixture turns dark brown—but do not allow it to burn.

3. Add the ginger, garlic, flour, cumin, coriander, and turmeric and cook over low heat, stirring constantly, for 5 minutes. Mix in 1 cup of the purée and whisk this mixture into the saucepan. Bring to a boil and remove from the heat. Add salt and pepper to taste, whisk in the yogurt, and serve immediately in heated bowls.

RED SNAPPER CHOWDER

This soup should be served as a main course. You can substitute a cheaper white-fleshed fish for the snapper, such as flounder, sea bass, or haddock, but the soup won't be as delicate.

— SERVES 6 —

1 medium onion, sliced

2 celery stalks with leaves, chopped

1 carrot, peeled and cut in 2-inch pieces

4 sprigs parsley

1 bay leaf

1 teaspoon dried thyme

3 pieces fresh orange rind, each about 2 inches by 1 inch

2 cups dry white wine

10 black peppercorns

1 tablespoon salt

2 1½-pound red snappers, cleaned, but with head and tail intact

1 cup canned Italian tomatoes, drained, seeded, and roughly chopped

4 tablespoons butter

1 medium onion, finely chopped

2 leeks, white part only, cleaned and chopped

1 clove garlic, minced

2 large potatoes, peeled and diced

Salt and freshly ground pepper

Garnish: chopped fresh basil or parsley

1. In a stockpot, combine the sliced onion, celery, carrot, parsley, bay leaf, thyme, orange rind, wine, 8 cups of water, the peppercorns, and salt. (The pot must be large enough to hold the fish, which will be added later.) Bring to a boil, then lower the heat and simmer, partially covered, for 30 minutes. Let cool for 30 minutes.

2. Add the fish to the stock and bring to a boil over high heat. Lower the heat immediately and simmer, partially covered, for 10 minutes, or until the fish flakes when tested with a fork. Remove from the heat and let stand in the stock for 15 minutes.

3. Using a slotted spoon, remove the fish from the stock. Cut off the heads and tails, remove the backbones, and return these to the stock. Reserve the fish flesh. Add the tomatoes to the stock and bring to a boil. Reduce to a simmer and cook, uncovered, for 45 minutes. Strain the stock through a sieve into a bowl.

4. While the stock is simmering, skin the fish flesh and flake it into a bowl. Dribble a few tablespoons of stock over the fish, cover, and reserve.

5. In a large saucepan, heat the butter, add the leeks and the chopped onion, and sauté over medium-low heat until soft. Add the garlic for the last minute of cooking. Add the stock and potatoes, bring to a boil, and simmer, uncovered, until the potatoes are tender, about 30 minutes.

6. Using a slotted spoon, remove about one third of the potatoes and purée them in a food mill. Add the purée to the soup with the reserved fish and heat through. Add salt and pepper to taste. Serve in heated bowls and garnish with chopped fresh basil or parsley.

SALT COD BOUILLABAISSE

This recipe is particularly useful if you live in a part of the country where a variety of fish is not readily available. For a richer, spicier soup, serve with a dollop of Rouille (page 83) in each bowl.

—— SERVES 6 ——

1 pound salt cod fillets

6 tablespoons olive oil

1 large onion, finely chopped

2 leeks, white part only, cleaned, cut in half lengthwise, and sliced

3 cloves garlic, minced

2 cups canned Italian tomatoes, drained, seeded, and chopped

2 cups dry white wine

8 cups White Fish Stock (page 7) or water

1 bay leaf

½ teaspoon dried basil

¼ teaspoon fennel seeds, crushed

¼ teaspoon saffron

1 piece fresh orange rind (about 2 inches)

1 teaspoon salt

Freshly ground pepper

2 large potatoes, peeled, cut in half, and thinly sliced

Garnish: chopped fresh parsley and Croutons (page 35)

1. Wash the salt cod fillets in cold water. Place them in a bowl, cover with cold water, and let them soak in the refrigerator, changing the water several times, for 24 hours. Cut the cod into 1-inch pieces, remove any skin and bones, and set aside.

2. In a large saucepan, heat the olive oil, add the onion and leeks, and sauté over medium-low heat until tender. Add the garlic for the last minute of cooking.

3. Add the tomatoes, raise the heat to moderate, and cook, stirring occasionally, for 5 minutes. Add the wine, raise the heat to high, and boil the liquid for 2 to 3 minutes.

4. Add the stock or water, bay leaf, basil, fennel seeds, saffron, orange rind, salt, and pepper to taste and bring the mixture

to a boil. Lower the heat and simmer, partially covered, for
30 minutes.

5. Add the potatoes and simmer, partially covered, until they are
tender, about 30 minutes.

6. Add the salt cod and cook at a low simmer, uncovered, for
10 minutes. Add more salt and pepper to taste.

7. Remove the bay leaf and orange rind. Serve in heated bowls,
garnish with the chopped fresh parsley, and serve the croutons
on the side.

ESCAROLE AND MEATBALL SOUP

— SERVES 8 —

1 slice of bread, crust removed

½ cup milk

½ pound lean ground beef

1 egg, lightly beaten

3 cloves garlic, minced

1 teaspoon salt

¼ teaspoon freshly ground pepper

½ teaspoon dried basil

¼ cup finely chopped fresh parsley

¼ cup freshly grated Parmesan, plus more for serving

1 teaspoon lemon juice

3 tablespoons olive oil

1 medium onion, finely chopped

1 celery stalk, finely chopped

¾ cup canned Italian tomatoes, drained, seeded, and chopped

1 head escarole (about 1 pound), shredded into ½-inch strips

10 cups Beef Stock (page 6)

Salt and freshly ground pepper

½ cup boxed Italian spaghetti, broken into 2-inch pieces

1. Tear the bread into pieces and soak in the milk. When soft, squeeze out the milk. In a bowl, combine the bread, beef, egg, 1 minced garlic clove, ½ teaspoon of the salt, the pepper, basil, parsley, Parmesan cheese, and lemon juice. Put the mixture in a food processor and blend, pulsing about 6 times. Chill the mixture, covered, for 2 hours.

2. Shape the chilled meat mixture into small balls, each 1 inch in diameter. You should have about 35 meatballs. Cover and chill while preparing the soup.

3. In a large saucepan, heat the oil, add the onion and celery, and sauté over medium-low heat until soft. Add the remaining 2 minced garlic cloves for the last minute of cooking. Add the tomatoes, the remaining ½ teaspoon of salt, and the escarole and cook for 2 to 3 minutes, stirring. Add the stock and bring to a boil. Lower the heat and simmer, partially covered, for 10 minutes. Add salt and pepper to taste.

4. Stir in the spaghetti and simmer, uncovered, for 5 minutes. Add the meatballs and simmer for 10 minutes, or until they rise to the surface. Remove 1 meatball and check to see that it is done.

5. Serve in heated bowls, with additional grated Parmesan on the side.

PORTUGUESE KALE AND LINGUICA SOUP

— SERVES 6 —

1 cup dried red kidney beans

1 pound fresh kale or one 10-ounce box frozen kale, defrosted

3 tablespoons olive oil

2 medium onions, finely chopped

3 cloves garlic, minced

4 medium potatoes, peeled and diced

8 cups Chicken Stock (page 5)

3 cups canned Italian tomatoes, drained, seeded, and chopped

1 bay leaf

1 teaspoon salt, plus more to taste

¾ pound linguica or chorizo sausage

Freshly ground pepper

1. Soak the beans overnight in water to cover. Drain the beans, place in a large saucepan, and cover with water. Bring to a boil, then lower the heat and simmer, partially covered, until tender, about 2 hours. Drain and reserve.

2. Wash the kale and strip the leaves from the stems. Discard the stems. Chop the leaves very fine. If using frozen kale, squeeze out excess liquid and chop very fine.

3. In a large saucepan, heat the oil, add the onions, and cook over medium-low heat until soft. Add the garlic for the last minute of cooking.

4. Add the potatoes, stock, tomatoes, bay leaf, and salt and bring to a boil. Lower the heat and simmer, partially covered, until the potatoes are very soft, about 30 minutes.

5. Meanwhile, prick the sausages, place them in a skillet, and cover with water. Bring to a boil, then lower the heat and simmer, uncovered, for 15 minutes. Drain on paper towels and slice into ¼-inch rounds.

6. With a wooden spoon, mash most of the potatoes against the side of the pan to make a coarse purée and blend into the soup.

7. Bring the soup to a simmer. Add the kale and simmer for 5 minutes. Add the sausage and the reserved beans and simmer until heated through. Remove the bay leaf and add salt and pepper to taste. Serve in heated bowls.

MINESTRONE

½ cup dried Great Northern beans (marrow beans are better, but difficult to find)

8 cups Chicken Stock (page 5)

1 ham shank, the smokier the better

2 medium potatoes, peeled and diced

4 cloves garlic, minced

1 medium onion, chopped

2 tablespoons olive oil

3 leeks, with 1 inch of green, cleaned and finely chopped

2 tablespoons chopped fresh parsley

1 tablespoon chopped fresh basil (or 1 teaspoon dried basil)

1 tablespoon chopped fresh summer savory (or 1 teaspoon dried summer savory)

2 carrots, peeled and cut into ¼-inch slices

1 turnip, peeled and cut into large dice

½ parsnip, peeled and cut into large dice

2 celery stalks, chopped

2 medium zucchini, cut into ½-inch slices

½ head chicory, shredded

½ head broccoli, florets only, chopped

½ fennel bulb, chopped

3 Jerusalem artichokes, peeled and chopped

6 Brussels sprouts, quartered

2 tablespoons tomato paste

2 teaspoons Dijon mustard

Salt and freshly ground pepper

Garnish: crumbled Gorgonzola cheese

1. Soak the beans overnight in water to cover. Drain the beans, place them in a large saucepan, and add the stock, ham shank, potatoes, 2 cloves of the garlic, and onion. Bring to a boil, then lower the heat and simmer, covered, for 1½ hours. Turn off the heat and remove the ham shank. Cut the meat into small pieces and return it to the pan.

2. In a skillet, heat the oil, add the leeks and the remaining 2 garlic cloves, and sauté for 5 minutes, then add the parsley, basil, and savory. Stir well and remove from the heat.

3. Bring the stock mixture to a boil over high heat and stir in the leek mixture with the remaining vegetables, tomato paste, and mustard. Add salt and pepper to taste. Lower the heat to medium and cook for 15 to 20 minutes. Serve in heated bowls and garnish with the crumbled Gorgonzola cheese.

HARIRA

Harira is to Moroccan cooking what minestrone is to Tuscan and onion soup is to French. Although eaten year round, it is part of the traditional fare of Ramadan, the month of fasting in the Arab world. This recipe was collected by Paula Wolfert, who writes, "Harira is peppery and lemony, rich with vegetables and meat and thickened with tedouira—a mixture of yeast or flour and water."

—— SERVES 6-8 ——

2 tablespoons butter

1 small onion, chopped

1 cup chopped fresh parsley

1 tablespoon celery leaves, finely chopped

1 teaspoon freshly ground pepper

1 teaspoon turmeric

½ teaspoon ground cinnamon

½ pound shoulder of lamb, cut into ½-inch cubes

Wings, back, and giblets of 1 chicken

½ cup dried lentils

2 tablespoons chopped cilantro

Salt

2 pounds tomatoes, peeled, seeded, and puréed

½ cup fine soup noodles

2 eggs beaten with the juice of half a lemon

Garnish: lemon wedges

1. In a stockpot, heat the butter over medium heat. Add the onion, parsley, celery leaves, pepper, and turmeric and sauté for 3 to 4 minutes, stirring frequently. Add the cinnamon, lamb, and chicken parts and cook slowly, turning the mixture over and over until golden but not browned, 15 to 20 minutes.

2. Meanwhile, pick over and wash the lentils. With a mortar and pestle, pound the cilantro leaves with a little salt into a paste or purée the leaves in a food processor with a spoonful of water. Add the lentils, cilantro paste, and puréed tomatoes to the pot. Cook over low heat for 15 minutes, then pour in 1½ quarts of water and cook until the lentils are soft and the soup is well blended, about 1 hour.

3. About 5 minutes before serving, add salt to taste and stir in the noodles. Bring to a simmer, cook for 2 minutes, and pour the egg and lemon mixture into the soup. Turn off the heat immediately and stir rapidly to form long egg strands. Serve at once, garnished with the lemon wedges.

CORN CHOWDER

This is a piquant variation on the American classic. It is best made in the summer months, when local corn is available.

—— SERVES 8 ——

4 slices of bacon

1 medium onion, finely chopped

3 celery stalks, finely chopped

4 cups Chicken Stock (page 5)

2 large potatoes, peeled and cubed

1 bay leaf

3 cups milk

5 large ears corn, kernels cut off the cob

1 cup sour cream, at room temperature

1 teaspoon lemon juice

Salt

Cayenne pepper

Garnish: bacon, chopped sweet red bell pepper, and chopped fresh parsley

1. In a large saucepan, cook the bacon until crisp. Drain on paper towels, crumble, and set aside.

2. Discard all but 3 tablespoons of the bacon fat from the pan. Heat the fat over medium-low heat, add the onion and celery, and sauté until soft but not brown. Add the stock, potatoes, and bay leaf and bring to a boil. Lower the heat and simmer, covered, until the potatoes are tender, about 30 minutes.

3. With a wooden spoon, roughly mash about half of the potatoes against the side of the pot and blend them into the soup.

4. Add the milk and corn, bring to a simmer, and cook until the corn is tender, about 5 minutes.

5. In a small bowl, beat a ladleful of the hot liquid into the sour cream. Whisk this into the hot soup, stirring. Add the lemon juice and salt and cayenne to taste. Remove the bay leaf. Serve in heated bowls and garnish with the bacon, chopped sweet red bell pepper, and chopped fresh parsley.

BORSCHT

This borscht should not be served cold. It is a filling soup and makes an ideal meal when served with salad, a loaf of black bread and unsalted butter, and a medium-body California zinfandel.

— SERVES 6 —

10 medium beets

4 tablespoons butter

1 large onion, chopped

½ head savoy cabbage, chopped

1 small potato, peeled and chopped

3 cloves garlic, minced

1 cup canned Italian tomatoes, drained, seeded, and lightly smashed

2 cups Beef Stock (page 6)

Salt and freshly ground pepper

2 cups buttermilk

1 cup sour cream, at room temperature

Garnish: chopped fresh dill

1. In a saucepan, cook the beets in boiling water for about 40 minutes, or until tender; run under cold water and peel off the skins. Chop and set aside.

2. In a large saucepan, heat the butter, add the onion, cabbage, potato, and garlic, and cook over medium heat for 5 minutes, or until the onion softens and the cabbage wilts. Add the beets and tomatoes and continue to cook over medium heat, stirring constantly, for 5 minutes. Add the stock and salt and pepper to taste and bring to a boil. Lower the heat and simmer for 1 hour.

3. Purée the soup in a food processor and return to the saucepan with the buttermilk. Bring the soup to a boil, remove from the heat, and whisk in the sour cream. Serve in heated bowls and garnish with the chopped fresh dill.

CHICKPEA SOUP WITH TOMATOES, ROSEMARY, AND GARLIC

We like the bite the red pepper flakes impart to this substantial soup, but if you have a delicate constitution you may want to reduce the amount.

— SERVES 6 —

2 cups dried chickpeas

4 cups Beef Stock (page 6) diluted with 4 cups water

1 bay leaf

½ cup olive oil

1 medium onion, finely chopped

4 cloves garlic, minced

2 teaspoons dried rosemary, crushed

½ teaspoon red pepper flakes

2 cups canned Italian tomatoes, drained, seeded, and finely chopped

½ cup freshly grated Parmesan

Salt and freshly ground pepper

1. Soak the chickpeas overnight in water to cover. Drain the chickpeas, place them in a large saucepan, and add the diluted stock and the bay leaf. Bring to a boil, then lower the heat and simmer, covered, until the chickpeas are tender, 1½ to 2 hours, depending on the age of the chickpeas.

2. In a skillet, heat the oil, add the onion, and sauté over medium-low heat until tender. Add the garlic, rosemary, and red pepper flakes and cook briefly. Add the tomatoes and simmer for 30 minutes.

3. When the chickpeas are tender, remove the bay leaf and any loose skins that have risen to the top. Purée about two thirds of the chickpeas in a food processor or food mill. Return to the pot. The soup should be quite thick—almost the consistency of a vegetable purée. If it seems too thick, thin it with stock or water. Add the tomato mixture and bring the soup to a simmer.

4. Remove from the heat and stir in the grated Parmesan and salt and pepper to taste. Serve in heated bowls.

RUSSIAN CABBAGE
AND SAUERKRAUT SOUP

¼ cup bacon fat

1 large onion, chopped

1 celery stalk, chopped

1 carrot, peeled and chopped

1 parsnip, peeled and chopped

2 cloves garlic, minced

1 pound sauerkraut

1 small savoy cabbage, quartered and shredded

8 cups Beef Stock (page 6)

1½ cups canned Italian tomatoes, drained well, seeded, and chopped

1 pound beef, chuck or round, cut into bite-size cubes

1 tablespoon sugar

2 tablespoons red wine vinegar

1 cup dry white wine

Salt and freshly ground pepper

Garnish: sour cream and chopped fresh dill

1. In a large saucepan, heat the bacon fat, add the onion, and sauté for 5 minutes. Add the celery, carrot, parsnip, and garlic and cook slowly for another 10 minutes.

2. Meanwhile, rinse the sauerkraut under cold water, squeeze out as much of the water as possible, and add the sauerkraut to the saucepan. Cook for another 3 minutes. Add the cabbage and continue cooking until the cabbage wilts.

3. Add the stock, tomatoes, and beef. Bring to a boil, then lower the heat and simmer, partially covered, for 45 minutes.

4. Add the sugar, vinegar, wine, and salt and pepper to taste. Cover and simmer for 1½ hours. Serve in large heated bowls and garnish with a dollop of sour cream and the chopped fresh dill.

LENTIL SOUP

5 tablespoons olive oil

2 medium onions, chopped

2 celery stalks with leaves, chopped

2 carrots, peeled and chopped

2 teaspoons ground cumin

2 cloves garlic, minced

1 pound lentils, rinsed

2 smoked ham hocks (about 1 pound) or 1 ham bone, preferably smoked

9 cups Chicken Stock (page 5) or water

1 bay leaf

1 cup canned Italian tomatoes, with liquid, chopped

1 pound fresh spinach, washed and chopped, or 1 10-ounce package frozen chopped spinach, defrosted and squeezed of excess liquid

Juice of 1 lemon

1 tablespoon salt

Freshly ground pepper

1. In a large saucepan, heat the olive oil, add the onion, celery, and carrots, and sauté over medium-low heat until soft. Add the cumin and garlic, stir, and sauté 1 minute longer.

2. Add the lentils, ham hocks, stock or water, bay leaf, and tomatoes and bring to a boil. Lower the heat and simmer, partially covered, until the lentils are tender, about 1 hour.

3. Remove the ham hocks and shred the meat, removing all fat and gristle. Reserve the meat.

4. Purée about half the lentils and return to the pan.

5. Add the ham, the spinach, lemon juice, salt, and pepper to taste and simmer for 15 minutes. Serve in heated bowls.

WHITE BEAN AND OXTAIL SOUP

*Oxtails make a very heavy stock, which is superb with legumes.
The resulting soup is rich and creamy, perhaps the heartiest
of those collected here.*

— SERVES 10 —

1 pound dried white Great
Northern beans

½ cup olive oil

2 pounds oxtails, cut into
2-inch slices

1 celery stalk, cut into thirds

1 carrot, cut into thirds

1 large onions, stuck with
2 cloves

2 bay leaves

1 large onion, finely chopped

2 leeks, white part only,
cleaned and thinly sliced

4 cloves garlic, minced

2 teaspoons Hungarian
paprika

1 cup canned Italian tomatoes,
drained, seeded, and
chopped

1 teaspoon dried marjoram

Salt and freshly ground pepper

Garnish: chopped fresh
parsley

1. Soak the beans overnight in cold water to cover. Drain and set
aside.

2. In a large saucepan, heat 3 tablespoons of the oil, add the oxtail
pieces, and brown on both sides.

3. Add 10 cups of water, bring to a boil, and skim the scum as it
rises to the surface. Add the celery, carrot, the onion stuck with the
cloves, and the bay leaves. Simmer, partially covered, skimming as
necessary, for 30 minutes.

4. Add the beans and cook at a very low simmer, covered, until
tender, about 2 hours.

5. Remove the celery, carrot, onion, and bay leaves and discard.
Remove the oxtail pieces, shred the meat, and set aside. Using a

slotted spoon, remove about half of the beans and purée them in a food processor or food mill with a little of the liquid from the saucepan.

6. In a skillet, heat the remaining 5 tablespoons of oil. Add the chopped onion and leeks, and sauté over medium-low heat until tender. Add the garlic and paprika for the last minute of cooking. Add the tomatoes and marjoram and simmer, stirring occasionally, for 15 minutes.

7. Add the tomato mixture, shredded meat, and puréed beans to the saucepan and simmer for 15 minutes. Add salt (it will need quite a bit) and pepper to taste, stirring constantly. Serve in heated bowls and garnish with the chopped fresh parsley.

BLACK BEAN SOUP

1 pound dried black beans

5 slices of bacon

3 medium onions, chopped

1 green bell pepper, chopped

2 celery stalks, chopped

3 cloves garlic, minced

1 teaspoon ground cumin

1 teaspoon dried oregano

2 teaspoons Dijon mustard

¼ cup chopped fresh parsley

7 cups Chicken Stock (page 5)

1 ham bone

1 bay leaf

2 tablespoons red wine vinegar

¼ cup sherry

Juice of ½ lemon

Salt and freshly ground pepper

Garnish: chopped cilantro or fresh parsley

1. Soak the beans overnight in water to cover. Drain the beans and reserve.

2. In a heavy casserole, cook the bacon over medium heat until it is crisp and the fat is rendered. Add the onions, pepper, and celery and sauté until soft but not brown.

3. In a small bowl, mix the garlic, cumin, oregano, mustard, and parsley and stir into the onion mixture. Add ½ cup of the stock and cook over medium heat, stirring constantly, for 10 minutes. Add the beans, the remaining 6½ cups of stock, the ham bone, and bay leaf, bring to a boil, and simmer, covered, for 1½ hours.

4. Remove the ham bone and bay leaf. Purée the mixture in a food processor or food mill and return to the casserole. Add the vinegar, sherry, lemon juice, and salt and pepper to taste and bring the soup to a simmer. Serve in warmed bowls and garnish with the chopped cilantro or fresh parsley.

SPLIT PEA SOUP

— SERVES 6-8 —

1 pound dried split green peas, rinsed and picked over

2 tablespoons butter

2 tablespoons olive oil

1 carrot, peeled and finely chopped

1 celery stalk, finely chopped

1 large onion, finely chopped

2 cloves garlic, minced

10 cups Chicken Stock (page 5)

2 medium potatoes, peeled and finely diced

2 smoked ham hocks or 1 ham bone

1 bay leaf

¼ teaspoon dried thyme

Freshly ground pepper

1. Soak the peas overnight in water to cover. Drain the peas and reserve.

2. In a large saucepan, heat the butter and oil over medium-low heat. Add the carrot, celery, and onion and sauté until soft. Add the garlic for the last minute of cooking.

3. Add the stock, split peas, potatoes, ham hocks, bay leaf, and thyme and bring to a boil. Lower the heat and simmer, partially covered, until the peas and potatoes are tender, 1 to 1½ hours.

4. Remove the bay leaf. Remove the ham hocks, shred the meat, removing all gristle, and set aside.

5. Purée the soup in a food processor or food mill and return to the pan. Add the ham and pepper to taste and simmer until heated through. Serve in heated bowls.

STEWS

M. F. K. Fisher has written, "A stew is supposed to be the simplest of dishes, and probably in the fargone days it was, when you threw a piece of meat and water into a pot, and let them boil together until they had blended into one edible thing. Now, a stew means something richer, and can be a fine, tantalizing dish indeed, full of braised meat, many vegetables, and all bound together by a gravy heady with herbs and wine."

There is hardly a national cuisine that does not employ the virtues that derive from an intermingling of aromas, flavors, and textures. We have tried to include a selection that reflects such variety of origin—you will find Moroccan Chicken Tagine with Prunes, Onions, and Almonds; Indian Keema with Peas; Mediterranean Fish Stew with Saffron and Rouille; Italian Braised Beef Shanks with Pine Nuts and Sultanas; and Chicken Mole from Mexico. As can be seen from even so brief a list, we are partial to the addition of dried fruits and nuts to braised meat. And chutneys satisfy this same predilection when combined with curries.

A few notes on procedure: although it takes time and attention, browning the meat properly is crucial to the flavor and texture of the meat and the quality of the sauce. Meat should be carefully dried before browning and should never be crowded in the pot. All stews, whether cooked on top of the stove or in the oven, should braise at the gentlest simmer; keep an eye on your stove and adjust the heat accordingly. Your pot should always be a heavy one—our preference is an enameled cast-iron casserole—that will accommodate the ingredients comfortably without too much extra space. Most stews can be made a day ahead and actually improve with standing; this also allows you to remove any excess fat that congeals on the top. As noted earlier, you should use no wine for a braising liquid that you would not serve your friends in a glass.

When the meat, vegetables, and herbs are finally assembled in a single pot, the cover placed atop, and the ingredients are gently simmering together in a savory liquid, one may settle in a neighboring room with a book only to be subtly distracted by the effluvial currents of air that carry on them the anticipation of pleasures to come from this harmonious transformation.

MEDITERRANEAN FISH STEW WITH SAFFRON AND ROUILLE

The following are good fish to use for this dish, and most are readily available in fish stores: haddock, halibut, whiting, pollack, red snapper, sea trout, striped bass, sea bass, grouper, hake, cod, perch, and whiting. For something a little special, add ½ pint of bay scallops (or sea scallops, quartered). In the classic Mediterranean bouillabaisse, many different fish are included—the more varieties, the tastier the soup. If you have a good fish store, have the fishmonger fillet the fish and use the bones and heads for the stock and the flesh for the soup itself. If possible, use one small whole mackerel, which will add welcome body and flavor to the soup.

— SERVES 6 —

STOCK

3 cups dry white wine

1 bay leaf

2 medium onions, quartered

¼ teaspoon dried oregano

2 celery stalks, chopped

5 sprigs parsley

2 carrots, peeled and chopped

2 teaspoons fennel seeds

2 pounds fish bones, including fish heads, and one small whole mackerel

¼ cup olive oil

1 large onion, chopped

1 leek, with 1 inch of green, cleaned and chopped

1 celery stalk, chopped

4 cloves garlic, finely chopped

¼ cup chopped fresh parsley

¼ teaspoon saffron

¼ teaspoon dried oregano

1 bay leaf

¼ teaspoon red pepper flakes

2 cups canned Italian tomatoes, drained, seeded, and chopped

2 fresh tomatoes, diced

1 medium potato, peeled and diced

1 piece orange rind

(continued)

2 pounds fish, cut into 1½-inch pieces

Garnish: Rouille (recipe follows)

1. For the stock: In a stockpot, combine the first nine ingredients plus 3 cups of water and bring to a boil. Lower the heat and simmer for 30 minutes. Strain and reserve.

2. In a large casserole, heat the oil over medium heat. Add the onion, leek, celery, garlic, parsley, saffron, oregano, bay leaf, and red pepper flakes and saute until the onion and celery have softened.

3. Add the stock, heated, canned and fresh tomatoes, potato, and orange rind, bring to a boil, and simmer for 50 minutes.

4. Add the fish and cook for 8 minutes.

5. Remove the bay leaf and the orange rind. Serve the stew with a small spoonful of rouille in each bowl and with the remaining rouille in a serving bowl on the side.

ROUILLE

2 dried hot red peppers

1 2-inch slice of French bread, crust removed

½ cup White Fish Stock (page 7) or water

5 cloves garlic, minced

½ sweet red pepper, roasted, peeled, and chopped (see page 276)

1 tomato, peeled, seeded, and chopped

1 pinch saffron

2 egg yolks

Salt and freshly ground pepper

¼ cup olive oil

1. Soak the dried hot peppers in boiling water for 10 minutes, or until they soften. Drain, seed, and place in a food processor.

2. Soak the bread in the stock or water, and squeeze out the excess liquid. Add to the processor.

3. Add the garlic, sweet red pepper, tomato, saffron, egg yolks, and salt and pepper to taste and blend until smooth. Add the oil slowly in a thin stream, allowing the mixture to thicken. Transfer to a serving bowl and refrigerate, covered, until ready to use.

PAELLA À LA VALENCIANA

This classic rice dish from Spain is prepared in as many ways as there are people who cook it. The following is Penelope Casas's version, of which she writes, "This is the rice dish that has achieved world renown—and justly so, for when it is well prepared it is truly a glorious dish. A medley of colors and tastes, this version has authentic flavor and is spectacularly beautiful."

— SERVES 8–10 —

6 cups very strong Chicken Stock (page 5)

½ teaspoon saffron

1 small onion

2 small chickens, about 2½ pounds each

Coarse salt

½ cup olive oil

¼ pound chorizo sausage, cut into ¼-inch slices

1 large pork chop, boned and diced

¼ pound cured ham, diced

1 medium onion, chopped

4 scallions, chopped

4 cloves garlic, minced

2 pimientos, diced

1 pound small or medium shrimp, shelled and deveined

2 live lobsters, split and divided into tail sections and claws; or 4 lobster tails, split lengthwise; or 8 king crab claws; or 8 jumbo shrimp, in their shells

3 cups short-grain rice (if possible, imported from Valencia; or use Italian arborio rice)

5 tablespoons chopped fresh parsley

2 bay leaves

½ cup dry white wine

1 tablespoon lemon juice

¼ pound fresh or frozen peas

Salt

18 small hard-shelled clams, scrubbed

18 small mussels, scrubbed

Garnish: lemon wedges and chopped fresh parsley

1. In a saucepan, bring the stock with the saffron and the whole onion to a boil, cover, and simmer for 15 minutes. Remove the onion and measure the stock—you will need exactly 5½ cups.

2. Cut the chickens into small serving pieces—the whole breast into 4 parts, each thigh into 2 parts, the bony tip of the leg chopped off, the wing tip discarded, and the rest of the wing separated into 2 parts. Dry the pieces well and sprinkle with the coarse salt.

3. In an ovenproof saucepan with about a 15-inch base, heat the oil. Add the chicken pieces and fry over high heat until golden. Set aside the chicken on a warm platter. Add the chorizo, pork, and ham to the pan and cook, stirring, for about 10 minutes. Add the chopped onion, scallions, garlic, and pimientos and cook until the onion softens.

4. Preheat the oven to 325°F.

5. Add the shrimp and the lobster and sauté for about 3 minutes, or until the shrimp and lobster barely turn pink. Remove the shrimp and lobster to the platter with the chicken.

6. Add the rice to the saucepan and stir to coat it well with the oil. Sprinkle in the parsley and add the bay leaves. (The dish may be made in advance up to this point.)

7. Add the reserved stock to the saucepan and bring to a boil. Stir it in with the wine, lemon juice, and peas. Add salt to taste and bring to a boil. Cook, uncovered, over medium-high heat, stirring occasionally, for about 10 minutes. Bury the shrimp and the chicken in the rice. Add the clams and the mussels, pushing them into the rice, with the edge that will open facing up. Top the paella with the lobster pieces. Bake, uncovered, for 20 minutes.

8. Remove from the oven and let sit on top of the stove, lightly covered with foil, for about 10 minutes. To serve, decorate with the lemon wedges and chopped fresh parsley.

JAMBALAYA

*Like its Creole cousin, gumbo, jambalaya can be made with a variety
of ingredients—all shellfish, for example, or all pork. We prefer this
more diverse collection, embracing shellfish, poultry, and pork, all in
a highly seasoned environment of rice and vegetables.*

—— SERVES 6–8 ——

4 cups Chicken Stock (page 5)

1 large whole chicken breast, split

3 tablespoons olive oil

1 pound sausage, hot Italian or kielbasa, cut into 1-inch pieces

1 pound cooked ham, cut into ½-inch cubes

2 large onions, finely chopped

3 celery stalks with leaves, finely chopped

2 large green peppers, or 1 green and 1 red, finely chopped

2 cloves garlic, minced

2½ cups canned Italian tomatoes, drained, seeded, and roughly chopped

1 teaspoon dried oregano

½ teaspoon dried thyme

1 teaspoon dried basil

1 bay leaf

1½ teaspoons salt

½ teaspoon white pepper

¼ teaspoon cayenne pepper

1½ cups long-grain rice

½ cup chopped fresh parsley

1 pound medium shrimp, shelled and deveined

1. In a large saucepan, bring the stock to a boil. Add the chicken, lower the heat immediately, and simmer, partially covered, until the flesh is firm and juices run clear, about 20 minutes. Let the chicken cool in the stock. Remove the meat from the bone, tear into bite-size pieces, and reserve. Reserve the stock.

2. In a 5-quart enameled casserole, heat the oil over medium-high heat. Add the sausage and sauté for 10 minutes, until browned on all sides. Add the ham and sauté, stirring occasionally, for 5 minutes.

3. Add the onions, celery, and peppers and sauté over medium heat, stirring often, until the vegetables are soft, about 15 minutes.

4. Add the garlic and sauté for 1 minute. Add the tomatoes, herbs, and spices. Reduce the heat to low and cook, stirring occasionally, for 45 minutes.

5. While the tomatoes finish cooking, preheat the oven to 350°F.

6. Add the chicken meat and 2 cups of the reserved stock and bring to a boil. Stir in the rice and parsley, cover, and bake for 15 minutes, or until the rice is nearly tender.

7. Stir in the shrimp and bake for 5 minutes more, or until the shrimp are firm but still tender.

8. Serve immediately from the casserole.

DUCK, SAUSAGE, AND OKRA GUMBO

We first tasted this excellent dish at the Cajun restaurant in New York City. Michael Campbell, the head chef there, offered a version of this recipe, which we modified for home use.

—— SERVES 6–8 ——

One 5-pound duck, quartered

2 carrots, peeled and quartered

2 celery stalks, quartered

1 large onion, chopped

5 sprigs parsley

3 bay leaves

1 tablespoon black peppercorns

6 slices of bacon

½ cup flour

1 pound kielbasa, sliced lengthwise and cut into ½-inch slices

¼ pound ham, julienned

1 medium onion, quartered and sliced

2 green peppers, chopped

8 scallions, thinly sliced

2 cloves garlic, minced

½ cup dry red wine

1½ cups canned Italian tomatoes, drained, seeded, and chopped

¾ pound okra, trimmed and cut into ½-inch slices

½ teaspoon cayenne pepper, or to taste

1 teaspoon dried thyme

½ teaspoon mace

½ teaspoon allspice

Salt

1 tablespoon filé powder

1. In a large stockpot, cover the duck, carrots, celery, chopped onion, parsley, bay leaves, and peppercorns with water and bring to a boil. Lower the heat and simmer for 1 hour. Strain and reserve the stock. Set the duck aside and let cool. When the stock has cooled, refrigerate it to allow the fat to congeal for easy removal. Remove the meat from the duck carcass and break it up into bite-size pieces, discarding the skin and fat, and set aside.

2. In a large flameproof casserole, cook the bacon until crisp and drain on paper towels. Reserve 4 tablespoons of the bacon fat in the casserole. Add the flour and cook over low heat, stirring constantly, until the flour is dark brown, but not burned, about 30 minutes. Add the kielbasa and ham and cook for 3 or 4 minutes. Add the sliced onion, peppers, scallions, reserved bacon, and garlic. Cook, stirring occasionally, for 10 minutes, or until the vegetables have softened.

3. Add the wine and stock (there should be about 10 cups), blend well, and add the tomatoes, okra, cayenne, thyme, mace, allspice, and salt to taste. Bring to a boil and simmer the gumbo, partially covered, for 1½ hours. Add the reserved duck meat during the last 10 minutes of cooking. Correct the seasoning and remove from the heat. Stir in the filé powder, stir the stew thoroughly, and serve with long-grain rice.

CHICKEN MOLE

The chocolate in this classic Mexican dish makes for a very rich, somewhat mysterious, and delicious sauce. We first tasted mole in Cuernavaca, where it was prepared by a superb local cook, whose dark sauce was the consistency of heavy cream. We have been disappointed since by the watery versions served in many American Mexican restaurants, but have found that the sauce is not difficult to master at home.

—— SERVES 8-10 ——

4 tablespoons oil

1 tablespoon sunflower kernels

¼ cup sesame seeds

½ teaspoon cumin seeds

½ teaspoon aniseeds

1 cup blanched slivered almonds

½ cup raisins

½ teaspoon dried oregano

½ teaspoon cinnamon

¼ teaspoon ground cloves

½ teaspoon ground coriander

⅓ cup chili powder

1 cup canned Italian tomatoes, drained, seeded, and chopped

2 medium onions, chopped

3 cloves garlic, minced

1 teaspoon salt

Freshly ground pepper

1 tortilla, torn into small pieces

3 cups Chicken Stock (page 5)

2 ounces unsweetened baking chocolate, grated

4 whole chicken breasts, split

4 chicken thighs

4 chicken drumsticks

Garnish: chopped cilantro

1. In a small skillet, heat 1 tablespoon of the oil over medium heat. Add the sunflower kernels, sesame seeds, cumin seeds, aniseeds, and almonds and cook, stirring constantly, until the sesame seeds and almonds are golden, 2 or 3 minutes. Purée the mixture in a food processor.

2. Add to the processor the raisins, oregano, cinnamon, cloves, coriander, chili powder, tomatoes, onions, garlic, salt, pepper, the tortilla, and ½ cup of the stock and purée until smooth.

3. Transfer the purée to a saucepan. Stir in the remaining 2½ cups of stock, bring the sauce to a simmer, and add the chocolate. Cook the sauce at a gentle simmer, stirring occasionally, to melt the chocolate.

4. While the sauce is simmering, rinse the chicken quickly in cold water and dry with paper towels. In a large casserole, heat the remaining 3 tablespoons of oil over medium-high heat. Sauté the chicken in batches until each piece is golden brown on all sides. Set the pieces aside on a plate as they are done.

5. Put the chicken and any accumulated juices in a flameproof casserole, placing the dark meat on the bottom. Pour the sauce over the chicken. Simmer, covered, until the chicken is tender, about 30 minutes.

6. Place the chicken on a warm serving platter. Pour the sauce over the chicken, garnish with the chopped cilantro, and serve.

MURGH MASALA

This classic northern Indian dish, which we found in Julie Sahni's excellent book on that cuisine, is a perfect intermingling of tomato, onion, garlic, and ginger with those spices Westerners associate with "curry"—cardamom, cinnamon, turmeric, and cumin. The addition of cilantro as a final touch—bright green against the reddish-brown sauce—is a stroke of genius. Do not be put off by the prospect of skinning the chicken—it is very easy.

—— SERVES 8 ——

Two 3-pound chickens, cut into 8 pieces each, or cut-up legs and breasts in any combination

½ cup plus 2 tablespoons light vegetable oil

3 large onions, thinly sliced

2 tablespoons minced garlic

3 tablespoons finely chopped fresh ginger

2 cinnamon sticks, each 3 inches long

4 black (or 8 green) cardamom pods

1 tablespoon turmeric

1 teaspoon red pepper flakes

2½ cups puréed or finely chopped fresh ripe tomatoes; or 2 cups canned tomatoes, drained, seeded, and chopped

1 tablespoon coarse salt

2 cups boiling water

1 tablespoon cumin seeds

3–4 tablespoons chopped cilantro

1. Cut off the wing tips and pull the skin away from the chicken pieces, using a kitchen towel to get a better grip. The wing tips and skin may be saved for making stock. Pat the chicken dry.

2. Heat 2 tablespoons of the oil over high heat in a large heavy skillet, preferably one with a nonstick surface. When the oil is very hot, add the chicken pieces, a few at a time, and sear them until they are nicely browned on all sides. Continue to brown the chicken in batches, setting aside the pieces as they are done.

3. Add the remaining ½ cup of oil to the skillet with the onions. Reduce the heat to medium-low and sauté the onions until they turn light brown, stirring constantly, about 30 minutes.

4. Add the garlic and ginger and sauté for 5 minutes. Add the cinnamon sticks and cardamom pods and cook until the cardamom pods are slightly puffed and begin to brown, a couple of minutes. Add the turmeric and red pepper flakes and stir quickly for 10 to 15 seconds. Add the tomatoes, chicken, salt, and water. Stir to mix, basting the chicken with the liquid, lower the heat, and simmer, covered, until the chicken is very tender, about 45 minutes.

5. While the chicken is cooking, heat a small heavy frying pan over medium heat, add the cumin seeds, and toast, stirring constantly, until they are dark brown, about 5 minutes. Grind the seeds with a mortar and pestle.

6. By the time the chicken is tender, the sauce should have thickened to the consistency of beef stew. If it is too thin, reduce it over high heat for a few minutes. Let the dish stand for at least 1 hour, off the heat and covered, before serving.

7. When ready to serve, heat the stew thoroughly, remove the cinnamon sticks and cardamom pods, and add the roasted cumin and chopped cilantro.

CHICKEN TAGINE WITH PRUNES, ONIONS, AND ALMONDS

*This recipe was learned many years ago in Paul Bowles's
Tangier kitchen. Its unique combination of flavors makes this tagine
(North African stew) an unforgettable eating experience.*

— SERVES 8 —

Salt and freshly ground pepper

¼ cup freshly ground cumin

Two 3-pound chickens, cut
   into serving pieces

1 pound pitted prunes

1½ tablespoons cinnamon

8 tablespoons olive oil

4 large Spanish onions, sliced

2 teaspoons turmeric

1 tablespoon ground ginger

1 cup whole unblanched
   almonds

Garnish: chopped cilantro

1. Rub salt and pepper and the cumin under and over the skin of
the chicken pieces and let them stand, unrefrigerated, for 1 hour.

2. In a saucepan, cover the prunes with cold water and add the
cinnamon. Bring to a boil, remove from the heat, and let the
prunes soak for 1 hour.

3. In a large skillet, heat 3 tablespoons of the oil. Add the onions,
turmeric, ginger, and salt and pepper to taste and cook over
medium heat until soft but not brown. Remove from the heat.

4. In a large casserole, toast the almonds in 2 tablespoons of the oil
over medium heat, stirring constantly. Set aside on a paper towel.

5. In the same casserole, heat the remaining 3 tablespoons of oil
over medium heat and brown the chicken.

6. Add the onion mixture to the casserole.

7. Drain the prunes over a bowl and reserve the liquid.

8. Add ½ cup of the prune liquid to the chicken and onion mixture. Bring to a boil, then lower the heat and simmer, covered, for 25 minutes.

9. Add the prunes to the casserole and continue cooking until the chicken is tender but not overcooked, about 15 minutes. If the tagine looks dry, more of the prune liquid may be added.

10. Arrange the chicken and prunes in a deep serving platter and cover with the sauce. Sprinkle with the browned almonds and the chopped cilantro and serve.

CHICKEN WITH MUSHROOMS AND ARTICHOKES

— SERVES 8-10 —

2 ounces dried porcini mushrooms

1 cup hot water

4 whole chicken breasts, about 1 pound each, split

4 chicken thigh and drumstick pieces, disjointed

2 teaspoons dried thyme

Salt and freshly ground pepper

3 tablespoons olive oil

3 tablespoons butter

3 medium onions, finely chopped

1 celery stalk, finely chopped

2 cloves garlic, minced

1 cup dry white wine

Juice of 1 lemon

2 cups canned Italian tomatoes, drained, seeded, and chopped

2 bay leaves

One 10-ounce package frozen artichokes, defrosted and sliced

Garnish: chopped fresh basil or parsley

1. In a small bowl, cover the dried mushrooms with the hot water and let soak for 1 hour. Remove the mushrooms from the water, chop finely, and set aside. Strain the liquid through a sieve lined with several layers of cheesecloth. Reserve the mushrooms and liquid.

2. Rinse the chicken quickly in cold water and dry with paper towels. Sprinkle with the thyme and salt and pepper to taste.

3. In a heavy skillet, heat the oil and 2 tablespoons of the butter. Add the chicken and sauté in batches over medium-high heat, until brown on both sides. Remove the chicken to a large flameproof casserole, placing the dark meat on the bottom.

4. When the chicken is done, remove all but 4 tablespoons of fat from the skillet. Add the onions and celery and sauté over medium-low heat, until soft and lightly browned. Add the garlic

for the last minute of cooking. Add the wine and reduce over high heat for 5 minutes, or until about ½ cup of liquid remains. Add the mushrooms and their liquid, the lemon juice, tomatoes, and bay leaves and simmer for 10 minutes.

5. Pour the onion/wine mixture over the chicken in the casserole. Bring to a simmer, cover, and cook slowly for 20 minutes, basting the chicken occasionally. Add the artichokes and continue cooking until the chicken is tender, about 10 minutes more.

6. Using a slotted spoon, remove the chicken to a heated platter. If the sauce is too thin, reduce it over high heat for a few minutes. Remove from the heat, swirl in the remaining tablespoon of butter, and pour the sauce over the chicken. Remove the bay leaves and garnish with the chopped fresh basil or parsley.

CHICKEN WITH WALNUTS, SHALLOTS, AND CREAM

—— SERVES 6-8 ——

1 cup walnut pieces

2 whole chicken breasts, split

4 chicken thigh and drumstick
pieces, disjointed

2 tablespoons butter

2 tablespoons walnut oil

30 medium shallots, peeled

1 cup dry white wine

Salt and freshly ground pepper

½ teaspoon dried tarragon

1 cup Chicken Stock (page 5)

½ cup heavy cream

1. Grind ½ cup of the walnuts in a food processor or blender and set aside.

2. Rinse the chicken quickly under cold water and dry with paper towels. In a large skillet, heat 1½ tablespoons of the butter and the oil over medium-high heat. Brown the chicken pieces in batches, setting them aside as they are done.

3. Pour off all but 2 tablespoons of fat. Add the shallots to the skillet and sauté over medium-low heat until lightly browned. Set aside.

4. Add the wine to the skillet and cook over high heat for a few minutes, scraping up the brown bits at the bottom of the skillet. Stir in the ground walnuts and return the chicken and any accumulated juices to the skillet, placing the dark meat on the bottom. Add the shallots, pushing them down into the wine/walnut mixture. Add salt and pepper to taste, sprinkle with the tarragon, and pour in the stock.

5. Bring the mixture to a simmer, cover, and cook slowly until the chicken is tender, about 30 minutes.

6. While the chicken is cooking, heat the remaining ½ tablespoon of butter over medium-high heat in a small skillet. Add the remaining walnut pieces and sauté for a few minutes, stirring constantly so they do not burn. Set aside.

7. When the chicken is tender, remove it and the shallots to a warmed serving dish.

8. Strain the sauce through a sieve into a small saucepan and reduce it over high heat until a little more than 1 cup remains. Add the cream, lower the heat, and boil gently until the sauce has thickened, 2 or 3 minutes. Pour the sauce over the chicken and top with the walnuts.

COQ AU VIN

*Of this classic dish, Michael Field wrote, "Coq au vin is simply
a chicken or, literally, a rooster stewed in wine. Each wine-
producing region of France has its own version but the Burgundian
coq au vin is the best known here. Ideally, it should be made with
the best Burgundy you can buy and the American types, though
lacking a certain robustness, should certainly be considered.
However, your coq au vin will only be as good as the wine it is
cooked in." The recipe that follows is from Michael Field; it is
the best coq au vin we've tasted, and we reproduce his recipe in
the very style in which it was originally written.*

—— SERVES 4 ——

One 3-pound frying chicken,
  disjointed (separate the
  joints cleanly with a knife
  rather than hacking through
  them with a cleaver)

Salt and freshly ground pepper

½ pound salt pork, cut into
  ¼-inch dice

5 tablespoons butter

12–16 little white onions, all
  approximately 1 inch in
  diameter, peeled and left
  whole

Vegetable oil, if needed

2 cups Burgundy

¼ cup brandy

2 tablespoons flour

½ cup Chicken Stock or Beef
  Stock (page 5 or 6)

BOUQUET GARNI

3 sprigs parsley

1 bay leaf

2 celery tops

½ teaspoon dried thyme

1 teaspoon salt

½ pound mushrooms

2 tablespoons finely chopped
  shallots

½ teaspoon finely chopped
  garlic

2 tablespoons finely chopped
  fresh parsley

1. Preheat the oven to 350°F.

2. Wash the pieces of chicken quickly under cold running water and dry them thoroughly with paper towels. Sprinkle the pieces liberally with salt and sparingly with pepper and put them aside while you prepare the salt pork and the white onions.

3. Blanch the diced salt pork in a little boiling water, drain, and pat it dry. In a large skillet, sauté the salt pork in 1 tablespoon of the butter until crisp and brown, then drain on paper towels. In the fat left in the skillet, brown the onions over medium heat, shaking the pan frequently so they will color evenly. Then transfer the onions to a shallow baking dish, add 3 tablespoons of the fat from the pan, and bake for about 30 minutes, turning the onions occasionally. Do not overcook. Remove the onions from the baking dish when done and put them aside in a bowl lined with a paper towel. Leave the oven on.

4. While the onions are baking (or, if you prefer, after they are done), heat the fat remaining in the frying pan, adding a couple of tablespoons of vegetable oil if there isn't enough fat to cover the bottom of the pan. Over fairly high heat, brown the chicken in this, starting the pieces skin side down and turning with kitchen tongs to brown each side. Each piece should be a deep golden brown when you finish.

5. While the chicken is browning, reduce the wine to 1½ cups by boiling it rapidly in an enameled or stainless steel pan.

6. When the chicken is brown, turn off the heat and, with a basting syringe, remove all but a thin film of fat from the pan. Warm the brandy and set it alight, stepping back as you do so. Pour the burning brandy over the chicken a little at a time, shaking the frying pan back and forth until the flame dies out. Transfer the chicken to a heavy 3- or 4-quart casserole with a closely fitting lid.

7. Stir the flour into the dark-brown glaze remaining in the frying pan, mixing it to a paste with all the fat and sediment you can

(continued)

scrape up from the bottom and sides of the pan. Add to this roux the reduced wine and the chicken or beef stock. Bring the mixture to a boil, stirring constantly with a wire whisk, and let it cook for a moment or two until it is smooth and thick. Strain the sauce through a fine sieve over the chicken in the casserole and add the bouquet garni, thyme, and the salt.

8. Now prepare the mushrooms. If they are large, slice or quarter them; if small, use them whole. Do not wash or peel them, but wipe them lightly with a moist towel and dry them thoroughly. Over medium heat, melt the remaining 4 tablespoons of butter in a large frying pan. When the foam subsides, add the chopped shallots and garlic; cook these together, stirring constantly for about 30 seconds before adding the mushrooms. Now raise the heat and, turning the mushrooms with a wooden spoon, cook them for no more than 2 or 3 minutes. Then, using a rubber scraper, add the mushrooms and all the pan juices to the chicken in the casserole.

9. Give the chicken a gentle turn or two with a large spoon so that the mushrooms, chicken, and herbs are all well moistened with the sauce. Then cover the casserole and bring the contents to a boil. At once, slide it onto the center shelf of the oven and bake, barely simmering, for 30 to 40 minutes, until it is tender. Add the baked onions to the casserole about 10 minutes before the chicken is done.

10. Coq au vin may be served directly from the casserole or, more impressively, on a platter, with the pieces of chicken arranged down the center and surrounded by mushrooms and onions. However you serve it, remove the bouquet garni from the sauce, and dust the surface of either the casserole or the platter with the chopped fresh parsley. Scatter the reserved salt pork scraps over the dish now, unless you prefer not to use them at all.

RABBIT STEW WITH PRUNES AND MUSHROOMS

You must allow one day for marinating the rabbit before you cook this savory stew. If you are using frozen rabbit—which we find acceptable—allow an additional two days for defrosting the rabbit in the refrigerator.

— SERVES 8 —

13 tablespoons olive oil

⅔ cup red wine vinegar

4 cloves garlic, minced

3 large onions, thinly sliced

1 tablespoon peppercorns, bruised

1 tablespoon juniper berries, bruised

2 bay leaves

1 teaspoon dried thyme

2 rabbits, 2½–3 pounds each, fresh or frozen, cut into serving pieces, with livers

3 cups dry red wine

1 tablespoon Dijon mustard

1 cup Chicken Stock (page 5)

3 tablespoons flour

Salt and freshly ground pepper

20 large pitted prunes

2 tablespoons butter

¾ pound fresh mushrooms, wiped clean and quartered

1. In a large glass bowl, combine 4 tablespoons of the oil, the vinegar, 2 garlic cloves, 1 onion, the peppercorns, juniper berries, 1 bay leaf, crumbled, and the thyme. Place the livers, covered, in the refrigerator. Toss the rabbit pieces in the marinade, cover, and refrigerate for 24 hours, turning the rabbit occasionally.

2. Remove the rabbit from the refrigerator a few hours before you intend to cook it and let it come to room temperature.

3. In a large heavy skillet, heat 3 tablespoons of the oil over medium-low heat. Add the remaining 2 onions and sauté until they are tender. Add the remaining 2 garlic cloves for the last minute of cooking. Transfer the onions to a flameproof casserole large enough to hold the rabbit.

4. Preheat the oven to 325°F.

5. Remove the rabbit from the marinade and dry with paper towels. Discard the marinade. Add 4 more tablespoons of oil to the skillet, raise the heat to medium high, and brown the rabbit pieces in batches, adding more oil if necessary. Transfer the browned pieces to the casserole as they are done. In the same skillet, sauté the rabbit livers until they are firm and browned but still slightly pink in the center. Chop the livers and set aside.

6. In a small saucepan, reduce the wine over high heat to 2 cups and set aside. Stir the mustard into the stock and set aside.

7. There should be 3 tablespoons of oil in the skillet in which you browned the rabbit and livers. Add more oil as necessary to make 3 tablespoons. Remove the pan from the heat and stir in the flour, making a paste with the oil. Put the skillet over medium-low heat and cook the flour, stirring constantly, until it is browned. Add the reduced wine and the stock with mustard and bring to a boil, stirring constantly with a whisk. Lower the heat and simmer until the sauce is smooth, about 5 minutes. Pour it over the rabbit in the casserole.

8. Add the remaining bay leaf and salt and pepper to taste to the casserole. Bring the casserole to a simmer, then cover and bake, basting occasionally, for 30 minutes. Add the prunes and return to the oven. Bake until the rabbit is tender, about 30 minutes more.

9. About 15 minutes before the rabbit is done, in a large skillet, heat the remaining 2 tablespoons of oil and 2 tablespoons of butter over medium-high heat. When the foam subsides, add the mushrooms and sauté them until lightly browned, about

10 minutes. Time this so that the mushrooms are finished at the same time the rabbit is done.

10. Place the rabbit pieces and mushrooms on a heated serving platter. Remove the bay leaf from the sauce and add salt and pepper to taste. Bring the sauce to a simmer, stir in the chopped liver, and pour the mixture over the rabbit and mushrooms.

RABBIT STEW WITH CABBAGE IN MUSTARD SAUCE

This dish is a variation on a recipe by Judie Geise. As with the preceding recipe, you must allow one day for marinating the rabbit and an additional two days for defrosting if you are using frozen rabbit.

— SERVES 8 —

2 rabbits, 2½–3 pounds each, fresh or frozen, cut into pieces

8 tablespoons Dijon mustard

2 cups dry red wine

2 cups dry sherry

1 large head cabbage, quartered and shredded

9 tablespoons butter

3 slices of lean bacon, sliced

1 cup plus 3 tablespoons flour

3 tablespoons paprika

Salt and freshly ground pepper

½ pound fresh mushrooms, quartered

2 medium onions, chopped

3 cloves garlic, chopped

1 cup light cream

¼ teaspoon red pepper flakes

Garnish: chopped fresh parsley

1. Coat the rabbit pieces with 5 tablespoons of the Dijon mustard and place in a large glass or ceramic bowl. Add the wine and sherry and refrigerate for 24 hours, turning the rabbit occasionally.

2. In a pot of boiling salted water, parboil the cabbage for 5 minutes. Drain under cold running water to stop the cooking process.

3. In a large flameproof casserole, heat 3 tablespoons of the butter, add the bacon, and cook until it just begins to crisp. Remove the bacon with a slotted spoon and reserve in a large bowl, leaving the rendered fat in the casserole.

4. Drain the rabbit and reserve the marinade. In a saucepan, reduce the marinade to 1 cup and set aside. Dry the rabbit with paper towels and toss the pieces in a bag filled with 1 cup of the flour, 2 tablespoons of the paprika, and salt and pepper to taste. Brown the rabbit, a few pieces at a time, in the reserved bacon fat in the casserole. Remove to a plate and set aside.

5. Preheat the oven to 325°F.

6. Melt another 3 tablespoons of the butter in the casserole and add the cabbage, mushrooms, onions, and garlic. Cook over medium-high heat for 15 minutes, mixing well. Remove to the bowl with the bacon.

7. Melt the remaining 3 tablespoons of butter in the casserole and whisk in the remaining 3 tablespoons of flour. Cook the mixture over low heat for 3 minutes, until lightly browned. Whisk in the reduced marinade and stir until it begins to thicken. Add the cream, the remaining 3 tablespoons of mustard, red pepper flakes, the remaining tablespoon of paprika, and salt and pepper to taste and cook for 2 or 3 minutes.

8. Layer the rabbit pieces, vegetables with the bacon, and the sauce in the casserole. Toss gently to distribute the ingredients, cover tightly, and bake until the rabbit is tender, about 1 hour. Garnish with the chopped fresh parsley.

VEAL STEW WITH SAUSAGE AND PEPPERS

3 pounds lean boneless veal, cut into 1½-inch cubes

1 cup dry red wine

1 cup plus 2 tablespoons flour

3 tablespoons paprika

Salt and freshly ground pepper

2 tablespoons vegetable oil

5 tablespoons butter

¾ pound hot Italian sausages, cut into ½-inch slices

½ pound fresh mushrooms, halved

2 leeks, with 1 inch of green, cleaned and finely sliced

1 medium onion, chopped

1 tablespoon sugar

2 cloves garlic, minced

3 carrots, peeled and sliced

1 yellow pepper, julienned

1 red pepper, julienned

1 green pepper, julienned

2 tomatoes, peeled, seeded, and chopped

1 tablespoon chopped fresh basil (or 1 teaspoon dried basil)

1 tablespoon chopped fresh thyme (or 1 teaspoon dried thyme)

¼ teaspoon freshly grated nutmeg

2 teaspoons Dijon mustard

1 tablespoon lemon juice

3 tablespoons finely chopped fresh parsley

½ cup dry white wine

¼ cup cognac

1 cup Chicken Stock (page 5) made with veal bones

Garnish: chopped fresh parsley

1. In a large bowl, cover the veal pieces completely with the red wine and let stand for 3 hours in the refrigerator. Drain, reserving the marinade. Dry the veal pieces with paper towels.

2. In another bowl, combine 1 cup of the flour, the paprika, and salt and pepper to taste.

3. In a large flameproof casserole, heat the oil and 2 tablespoons of the butter. Coat the pieces of veal with the seasoned flour, shaking off the excess, and brown the veal in the casserole, a few pieces at a time. (Flour the veal only when it is ready to be browned, so that the flour does not get soggy.) Remove the veal pieces to a large bowl as they are browned.

4. When all the veal has been browned, brown the sausage slices in the fat left in the casserole and add to the bowl with the veal.

5. Preheat the oven to 350°F.

6. In the casserole, heat the remaining 3 tablespoons of butter. Add the mushrooms, leeks, and onion and cook over high heat, stirring well to dislodge the brown bits in the casserole, for 3 minutes. Add the veal, sprinkle with the sugar, and cook for 5 minutes, stirring constantly, until the sugar has caramelized slightly. Lower the heat to moderate and add the garlic, carrots, peppers, and tomatoes. Sprinkle with salt and pepper to taste, add the remaining 2 tablespoons of flour, the basil, thyme, and nutmeg, and cook for 5 minutes, stirring constantly. Mix in the mustard, lemon juice, and parsley.

7. In a small saucepan, combine the red wine marinade, the white wine, and the cognac. Reduce the liquid over high heat to 1 cup and stir it into the casserole with the stock.

8. Bring the contents of the casserole to a boil, then cover and bake until the veal is tender but not overcooked, about 1 hour. Garnish with the chopped fresh parsley.

VEAL MARENGO

2 pounds boned leg of veal, cut into 1½-inch cubes

8 tablespoons butter

2 tablespoons olive oil

1 small onion, finely chopped

Salt and freshly ground pepper

2 tablespoons flour

1 cup dry white wine

1 cup Chicken Stock (page 5)

2 tomatoes, peeled, seeded, and chopped

1 cup canned Italian tomatoes, drained, seeded, and chopped

1 clove garlic, minced

½ teaspoon dried thyme

½ teaspoon dried tarragon

BOUQUET GARNI

4 sprigs parsley

1 celery stalk with leaves

1 small leek, cleaned and trimmed

1 bay leaf

½ pound fresh mushrooms, halved

12 small white onions

1 tablespoon sugar

Garnish: chopped fresh parsley

1. Preheat the oven to 325°F.

2. Pat the veal dry with paper towels. In a large flameproof casserole, heat 2 tablespoons of the butter and the oil over medium-high heat and quickly brown the veal, a few pieces at a time; reserve in a bowl. Add another 2 tablespoons of the butter to the casserole and sauté the onion until light brown. Sprinkle with the salt and pepper and the flour and cook for another 3 minutes over medium-high heat, to allow the flour to color lightly.

3. Return the veal to the casserole, add the wine, stock, fresh and canned tomatoes, garlic, thyme, tarragon, and bouquet garni. Bring to a boil, then cover and bake oven for 30 minutes.

4. Meanwhile, in a skillet, sauté the mushrooms in 2 tablespoons of the butter over medium-high heat for 3 or 4 minutes. Remove the mushrooms with a slotted spoon and set aside. In the same skillet, melt the remaining 2 tablespoons of butter, add the white onions, sprinkle them with the sugar, and sauté until golden brown, about 10 minutes.

5. When the stew has cooked for 30 minutes, add the mushrooms and white onions and bake until the veal is tender, about 40 minutes more. When ready to serve, taste for seasoning, remove the bouquet garni, and garnish with the chopped fresh parsley.

CHILI

Three 14-ounce cans of Goya small white beans

5 tablespoons chili powder

2 tablespoons ground cumin

1 tablespoon dried oregano

1 teaspoon red pepper flakes (or 1 hot red pepper, finely chopped)

1 teaspoon salt

1 teaspoon freshly ground black pepper

1 cup dry red wine

½ pound slab bacon, diced

4 medium onions, chopped

1 sweet red pepper, chopped

1 green pepper, chopped

6 cloves garlic, chopped

3 pounds ground chuck

½ pound sausage meat

4 tablespoons chopped cilantro

1½ cups canned Italian tomatoes, drained, seeded, and chopped

3 tablespoons tomato paste

1 ounce unsweetened baking chocolate, grated

1. Drain the beans, place in a large saucepan, and cover with cold water. Bring to a boil, lower the heat, and simmer, partially covered, until tender, about 2 hours. Drain and set aside.

2. In a small bowl, mix the chili powder, cumin, oregano, red pepper flakes, salt, and pepper and blend in the wine. Set the bowl aside for 5 or 10 minutes to let the spices dissolve in the wine.

3. In a heavy casserole, cook the bacon over medium heat until crisp. Add the onions, peppers, and garlic and sauté them until they begin to soften, about 5 minutes.

4. Add the chuck and sausage meat, breaking it up with a wooden spoon, and brown it lightly. Stir in the beans.

5. Lower the heat, add 2 tablespoons of the cilantro, the tomatoes, and tomato paste, and stir in the spice/wine mixture. When the ingredients are well combined, add the chocolate and mix thoroughly. Cover and simmer for 1 hour.

6. Mix in the remaining 2 tablespoons of cilantro and serve in heated bowls.

BOEUF BOURGUIGNON

*We have all been served travesties of this famous dish, but properly
prepared, its preeminence in the world of stews is justly deserved.
As Julia Child said, "Carefully done, and perfectly flavored, it is
certainly one of the most delicious beef dishes concocted by man"—
and if you follow her recipe below, it will be just that. We always
make it a day ahead of time and serve it with steamed new potatoes,
except on Christmas Eve, when we cover it with a crust of puff
pastry to make an elegant meat pie.*

— SERVES 6 —

One 6-ounce chunk of bacon

4½ tablespoons olive oil

3 pounds beef rump, chuck,
or round, cut into 2-inch
cubes

1 carrot, peeled and sliced

1 medium onion, sliced

Salt and freshly ground pepper

2 tablespoons flour

3 cups dry red wine

2–3 cups Beef Stock (page 6)

1 tablespoon tomato paste

2 cloves garlic, mashed

½ teaspoon dried thyme

1 bay leaf

5½ tablespoons butter

18–24 small white onions,
peeled

1 pound fresh mushrooms,
quartered

Garnish: chopped fresh
parsley

1. Preheat the oven to 450°F.

2. Remove the rind from the bacon and cut the bacon into lardons,
¼ inch by 1½ inches. Simmer the rind and bacon for 10 minutes in
1½ quarts of water. Drain and dry. Set the rind aside.

3. In a large enameled cast-iron casserole, sauté the bacon in
1 tablespoon of the oil over medium heat for 2 to 3 minutes, until
lightly browned. Remove to a side dish with a slotted spoon.

4. Dry the beef with paper towels. In the casserole, heat the bacon fat and oil until it is almost smoking, then sauté the beef, a few pieces at a time, until nicely browned on all sides, removing the beef as done and setting it aside with the bacon.

5. Reduce the heat to medium and brown the carrot and onion in the same fat. Pour the fat out of the casserole.

6. Return the beef and bacon to the casserole and toss with 1 teaspoon of salt and ¼ teaspoon of freshly ground pepper. Sprinkle on the flour and toss again to coat the beef. Set the casserole, uncovered, on the middle shelf of the oven for 4 minutes. Toss the meat and return to the oven for 4 minutes more. Remove the casserole and turn the oven down to 325°F.

7. Stir in the wine and enough stock so that the meat is barely covered. Add the tomato paste, garlic, thyme, bay leaf, and reserved bacon rind. Bring to a simmer, cover, and place in the lower third of the oven. Regulate the heat so that the liquid simmers very slowly for 3 to 4 hours. The meat is done when a fork pierces it easily.

8. While the beef is cooking, prepare the onions and mushrooms. Heat 1½ tablespoons of the butter and 1½ tablespoons of the olive oil over medium heat in a large skillet. When the butter and oil are bubbling, brown the white onions as evenly as possible, rolling them around for about 10 minutes. Pour in ½ cup of the beef stock and add salt and pepper to taste. Cover and simmer until the onions are tender but still retain their shape and the stock has evaporated, 40 to 50 minutes. Set aside until needed.

9. Place the remaining 4 tablespoons of butter and 2 tablespoons of the oil in another large skillet over high heat. As soon as you see that the butter foam has begun to subside, add the mushrooms and sauté until lightly browned. Set aside.

10. When the meat is tender, pour the contents of the casserole into a sieve set over a saucepan. Wash out the casserole and

(continued)

return the beef and bacon to it. Distribute the cooked onions and mushrooms over the meat.

11. Skim the fat off the sauce. Simmer the sauce for a minute or two, skimming off additional fat as it rises. You should have about 2½ cups of sauce thick enough to coat a spoon lightly. If too thin, boil it down rapidly. If too thick, mix in a few tablespoons of stock. Taste for seasoning and pour the sauce over the meat and vegetables.

12. Cover the casserole and simmer for 2 to 3 minutes, basting the meat and vegetables with the sauce. Garnish with the chopped fresh parsley and serve.

SAAG GOSHT

We first tasted this traditional Moghul dish at the Shezan restaurant in New York City and were so taken with the pungent blending of lamb, spinach, and spices that we ordered the dish on many return visits. Even more than with most stews, the individuality of the ingredients gives way to the luxuriousness of the finished whole. We usually serve Saag Gosht with Aromatic Rice (page 280), Eggplant Raita (page 279), and Tomato Chutney (page 283).

—— SERVES 8 ——

4 pounds fresh spinach or four 10-ounce packages of frozen chopped spinach, thoroughly defrosted

2 large onions, chopped

¼ cup chopped fresh ginger

8 cloves garlic, chopped

4 pounds boneless lamb shoulder, cut into 1½-inch cubes, fat removed

⅓ cup vegetable oil

2 bay leaves

8 whole cloves

8 cardamom pods

1 cinnamon stick

2 tablespoons ground coriander

1½ tablespoons ground cumin

1 teaspoon turmeric

½ teaspoon cayenne pepper

1 tomato, peeled, seeded, and chopped

¼ cup plain yogurt

2 teaspoons salt

1 tablespoon garam masala*

---

* Garam masala is a mixture of spices available at Indian grocery stores. It usually consists of cumin, cardamom, coriander seeds, cinnamon, cloves, and black pepper.

1. If you are using fresh spinach, wash it carefully, remove the thick stems, and place it in a large stainless steel pot with the

(continued)

water that still clings to the leaves from the washing. Cook over medium-low heat until the spinach is wilted, stirring occasionally. You may have to do this in batches if your pot isn't large enough. Drain and when the spinach is cool enough to handle, squeeze out the excess liquid and chop finely. If you are using frozen spinach, squeeze the excess liquid out of the defrosted spinach and chop it again. Set aside.

2. In a blender or food processor, combine the onions, ginger, and garlic, add ¼ cup of water, and blend until the vegetables have been puréed into a paste. If you use a blender, you may have to do this in batches. Set aside.

3. Dry the lamb with paper towels. In a casserole large enough to hold all the lamb (about a 7-quart capacity), heat the oil over medium-high heat and brown the meat on all sides in batches, removing it with a slotted spoon to a plate when done. Add more oil between batches if necessary.

4. Preheat the oven to 325°F.

5. When the lamb is browned, there should be a film of oil remaining in the casserole. Over medium heat, sauté the bay leaves, cloves, cardamom pods, and cinnamon stick until the cardamom pods swell, about 1 minute. Add the onion purée and sauté, stirring constantly, until the paste darkens, about 15 minutes. Stir in the coriander, cumin, and turmeric and sauté, stirring, for 1 or 2 minutes. Add the cayenne, tomato, and yogurt and sauté, stirring, for 5 minutes. Stir in 3 cups of water and the salt. Add the lamb and any accumulated juices, stir to distribute the sauce, and bring to a boil, then cover and bake for 1 hour.

6. Remove the casserole from the oven, add the spinach, and combine well. Return the casserole to the oven and continue baking, covered, until the meat is very tender, about 1 hour more.

7. When the meat is done, you should have a very thick sauce. If the sauce is too thin, put the casserole over high heat and cook until the sauce thickens. Remove the cloves, cardamom pods, and cinnamon stick. Stir in the garam masala, add salt to taste, and serve on a heated platter.

BRAISED BEEF WITH LEEKS, CARROTS, AND CELERY

— SERVES 8 —

¼ pound slab bacon, diced

2 tablespoons olive oil, plus more as needed

4 pounds beef chuck, cut into 1½-inch cubes

1 medium onion, finely chopped

4 leeks, cut in half lengthwise, cleaned, and sliced

5 carrots, peeled

5 celery stalks

2 garlic cloves, minced

3 tablespoons flour

4 cups dry red wine

1½ cups Beef Stock (page 6)

1 tablespoon tomato paste

½ teaspoon dried summer savory

1 bay leaf

Salt and freshly ground pepper

Garnish: chopped fresh parsley

1. Preheat the oven to 325°F.

2. In a small saucepan, cover the bacon with cold water, bring to a boil, lower the heat, and simmer for 5 minutes. Drain and dry on paper towels.

3. In a large skillet, heat the oil over medium-high heat, add the bacon, and sauté until it is nicely browned and has rendered most of its fat. Remove the bacon with a slotted spoon and set aside on paper towels.

4. In the fat that remains in the skillet, brown the beef in batches over medium-high heat, removing it with a slotted spoon to a large casserole as it is browned.

5. Reduce the heat to medium-low and sauté the onion, leeks, 1 carrot, finely chopped, and 1 celery stalk, finely chopped, until they are soft. Add the garlic for the last minute of cooking. Transfer the vegetables to the casserole.

6. There should be about 3 tablespoons of fat left in the skillet; if there is less, add some olive oil. Remove the skillet from the heat and stir the flour into the fat, forming a paste. Put the skillet over medium-low heat and cook the paste, stirring constantly, until it is browned. Dissolve the tomato paste in the wine and the stock, add it to the skillet, and bring to a boil, stirring constantly. Lower the heat and simmer for 5 minutes.

7. Add the sauce to the casserole. Stir in the reserved bacon, the summer savory, bay leaf, 1 teaspoon of salt, and pepper to taste. Bring the casserole to a simmer, then cover and bake for 2 hours.

8. While the stew is cooking, prepare the vegetables. Cut the remaining carrots into 1½-inch lengths, cutting the thicker pieces in half lengthwise. Cut the remaining celery stalks in half lengthwise and then into 1½-inch lengths.

9. When the meat has cooked for 2 hours, remove the casserole from the oven and stir in the vegetables. Continue baking until the meat is very tender and the vegetables are cooked but still firm, about 1 hour more.

10. Add salt and pepper to taste, garnish with the chopped fresh parsley, and serve from the casserole.

CARBONNADE À LA FLAMANDE

¼ pound slab bacon, finely diced

4 pounds boneless chuck roast, cut into 1½-inch cubes, fat removed

5 large onions, cut in half and thinly sliced

1 tablespoon brown sugar

2 cloves garlic, minced

3 tablespoons flour

1½ cups Beef Stock (page 6)

2 cups dark beer

2 tablespoons red wine vinegar

¾ teaspoon dried thyme

2 bay leaves

1 teaspoon salt

Freshly ground pepper

Garnish: chopped fresh parsley

1. In a large skillet, brown the bacon over low heat until all the fat is rendered. Drain the bacon on paper towels and reserve. Raise the heat to medium-high, dry the beef, and brown it in batches in the rendered fat, transferring it to a large flameproof casserole as it is done.

2. When the meat is browned, reduce the heat to medium-low. Add the onions to the skillet and cook them slowly, stirring occasionally, until soft, about 20 minutes. Stir in the sugar and cook, stirring often, for another 5 minutes. Add the garlic for the last minute of cooking. Transfer the onion mixture to the casserole with a slotted spoon.

3. Preheat the oven to 325°F.

4. There should be about 3 tablespoons of fat left in the skillet. Remove the skillet from the heat and stir the flour into the fat, forming a paste. Put the skillet over medium-low heat and cook the paste, stirring constantly, until it is browned. Slowly stir in the stock, beer, and vinegar and bring to a boil, stirring constantly. Lower the heat and simmer for 5 minutes.

5. Add the sauce to the casserole with the thyme, bay leaves, salt, and pepper to taste.

6. Bring the casserole to a simmer, then cover and bake until the meat is tender, about 3 hours.

7. Remove the bay leaves. With a slotted spoon, transfer the meat and onions to a heated serving platter. If the sauce is thin, reduce it quickly over high heat.

8. Add salt and pepper to taste. Pour the sauce over the meat and onions and garnish with the reserved bacon and the chopped fresh parsley.

BRAISED SHORT RIBS WITH ONIONS, MUSTARD, AND WHITE WINE

— SERVES 6 —

⅓ cup flour

Salt and freshly ground pepper

6 pounds beef short ribs, cut into single ribs, fat removed

¼ cup bacon fat

3 large onions, sliced

⅓ cup Dijon mustard

3 tablespoons tomato paste

2 cups dry white wine

½ teaspoon dried rosemary

½ teaspoon dried thyme

2 bay leaves

4 cloves garlic, minced

1. Preheat the oven to 300°F.

2. Mix the flour with ½ teaspoon of salt and pepper to taste and coat the ribs with it, shaking off the excess.

3. In a large casserole (about a 7-quart capacity), heat the bacon fat over medium-high heat and brown the ribs in batches. As they are done, remove them with a slotted spoon and set aside.

4. When the ribs have been browned, draw off all but about 3 tablespoons of fat from the casserole. Add the onions to the casserole and sauté over medium-low heat until they begin to soften, scraping up the brown bits at the bottom of the casserole.

5. While the onions are cooking, mix the mustard and tomato paste together and combine the mixture with the wine.

6. When the onions are soft, add the wine mixture and the short ribs to the casserole with the rosemary, thyme, bay leaves, 1 teaspoon of salt, and pepper to taste. Stir to distribute the ingredients and bring to a simmer, then cover and bake for 2½ hours, basting occasionally.

7. Fold in the garlic and bake, uncovered, until the meat is tender, about 30 minutes more.

8. When the meat is done, you should have a thick sauce. If the sauce is too thin, remove the ribs to a heated platter and reduce the sauce over high heat. Remove the bay leaves, pour the sauce over the meat, and serve.

BEEF STROGANOFF

—— SERVES 8 ——

2 ounces dried porcini
   mushrooms

1 cup hot water

2 tablespoons vegetable oil

7 tablespoons butter

5 shallots, chopped

½ pound fresh mushrooms,
   sliced

2 tablespoons flour

½ cup sherry

3 tablespoons lemon juice

2 tablespoons tomato sauce

1 cup Beef Stock (page 6)

1 teaspoon paprika

Salt and white pepper

1 cup sour cream

3 pounds sirloin or skirt steak,
   cut into ¼-inch slices

Garnish: **chopped fresh chives**

1. Cover the dried mushrooms with the hot water and let soak for 1 hour. Remove the mushrooms, mince, and set aside. Strain the liquid through several layers of cheesecloth into a bowl and reserve.

2. In a large flameproof casserole, heat 1 tablespoon of the oil and 2 tablespoons of the butter over high heat. Add the shallots and the fresh and soaked dried mushrooms and sauté for 4 or 5 minutes, allowing the mushrooms to brown slightly. Remove to a dish.

3. Melt 3 tablespoons of the butter in the casserole, mix in the flour, and cook over low heat until the roux just starts to color. Whisk in the sherry, a little at a time, and then the lemon juice, tomato sauce, stock, and reserved mushroom liquid and continue cooking until the sauce thickens. Stir in the paprika, salt and white pepper to taste, and the mushroom/onion mixture. Remove from the heat.

4. In a large skillet, melt the remaining 2 tablespoons of butter and 1 tablespoon of oil over medium-high heat and quickly brown the beef, making sure that the outside of the meat is well browned and the inside is pink. As the pieces are browned, remove them to the sauce.

5. When you are ready to serve, bring the stroganoff to a boil, remove from the heat, and stir in the sour cream. Garnish with the chopped fresh chives.

BRAISED BEEF SHANKS WITH PINE NUTS AND GOLDEN RAISINS

This is a classic Italian way of cooking oxtail. We prefer the beef shank because it's meatier and bears the additional delight of marrow. If you decide to use oxtail, be sure to get disks about 4 inches in diameter and 1 inch thick—the smaller pieces are good for soup but difficult to negotiate in a stew.

—— SERVES 6 ——

6 slices of beef shank, approximately 4 inches in diameter and 1 inch thick, with bone

8 tablespoons olive oil

1 large onion, chopped

1 carrot, peeled and finely chopped

3 cloves garlic, minced

2 cups dry white wine

1 cup canned Italian tomatoes, drained, seeded, and chopped

½ teaspoon salt

Freshly ground pepper

1 bay leaf

1 teaspoon dried marjoram

4 large celery stalks with leaves, cut into ½-inch slices

¼ cup pine nuts

⅓ cup golden raisins

⅓ cup boiling water

Garnish: chopped fresh parsley

1. Preheat the oven to 325°F.

2. Cut the membrane surrounding the slices of shank in several places so that the slices will lie flat when browned. In a large enameled flameproof casserole, heat 5 tablespoons of the oil over medium-high heat and sauté the beef in batches until it is nicely browned on both sides, adding oil as needed. Remove to a plate and reserve.

3. There should be about 3 tablespoons of oil left in the casserole. Add the onion and carrot and sauté over medium-low heat until soft. Add the garlic for the last minute of cooking.

4. Add the wine, tomatoes, salt, pepper to taste, bay leaf, marjoram, and beef to the casserole with any juices that have accumulated on the plate. Spoon the liquid, vegetables, and herbs over the meat. Bring the casserole to a simmer, then cover and bake, basting the meat occasionally, for 1½ hours. Add the celery and bake until the meat is very tender, about 1 hour more.

5. While the meat is cooking, put the pine nuts in a dry skillet and toast until golden, about 5 minutes, shaking the skillet occasionally to color them evenly. Set aside. Put the golden raisins in a small bowl, cover them with the boiling water, and let soak for 30 minutes. Drain and set aside.

6. When the meat is tender, remove it to a heated serving dish. Skim the fat from the surface of the sauce, stir in the pine nuts and golden raisins, and pour the sauce over the meat. Garnish with the chopped fresh parsley and serve.

PICADILLO

A dish in Cuban, Mexican, and Tex-Mex cuisines, picadillo *is one of the classic transformations of ground meat, simultaneously hot and sweet. If you like, make it hotter still by experimenting with different chilies.*

—— SERVES 6 ——

¾ cup golden raisins

½ cup hot water

1 tablespoon tomato paste

3 tablespoons oil

2 medium onions, finely chopped

1 green Anaheim chili pepper, seeded and finely chopped

4 cloves garlic, minced

1½ pounds ground pork loin

1½ pounds ground beef

1 cup drained green olives stuffed with pimentos, cut in half

¼ cup drained capers, rinsed

1 large green cooking apple, peeled, cored, and finely diced

2 tablespoons salt

½ teaspoon cinnamon

½ teaspoon ground cloves

1 teaspoon ground cumin

1 tablespoon chili powder

½ teaspoon dried oregano

1 bay leaf

¼ cup cider vinegar

6 tomatoes, peeled, seeded, and chopped

½ cup of your favorite salsa

½ cup chopped cilantro

Garnish: sour cream

1. Soak the golden raisins in the hot water for 30 minutes, then drain, reserving both the golden raisins and liquid. Dissolve the tomato paste in the liquid.

2. In a large skillet, heat the oil over medium-low heat, add the onions and pepper, and sauté until soft. Add the garlic for the last minute of cooking.

3. Add the pork and beef. Raise the heat to medium and cook, stirring to break up the lumps, until the meat is lightly browned.

4. Add the olives, capers, apple, salt, cinnamon, cloves, cumin, chili powder, oregano, bay leaf, vinegar, and tomato paste mixture and cook, uncovered, stirring occasionally, for 10 minutes.

5. Add the tomatoes and simmer, uncovered, stirring occasionally, for about 1¼ hours, or until the stew has thickened. Stir in the salsa, golden raisins, and cilantro 15 minutes before the stew is done. Serve with the sour cream on the side.

SHEPHERD'S PIE

This dish was often served for lunch at the Tangier house of Martin Hawes, an English colonial who spent his life exploring the native cuisines of Tibet, India, and Morocco. The shepherd's pie would usually be accompanied by boiled cauliflower, a salad of mixed greens, and a modest claret.

—— SERVES 6 ——

2 medium onions, chopped, plus ½ small onion, chopped

5 tablespoons butter

2 cloves garlic, finely chopped

1 celery stalk, finely chopped

1 pound ground lamb

1 pound ground beef

1½ cups canned Italian tomatoes, drained, seeded, and chopped

2 tablespoons flour

Salt and freshly ground pepper

1 teaspoon Bovril or Oxo Beef Cubes (concentrated beef extract)

½ teaspoon dried thyme

1 tablespoon Worcestershire sauce

1 bay leaf

½ cup chopped fresh parsley

½ cup chopped cilantro

4 large baking potatoes, peeled and cubed

¼ cup milk

½ cup freshly grated Parmesan

1. Preheat the oven to 325°F.

2. In a large skillet, sauté the 2 medium onions in 3 tablespoons of the butter over medium-low heat until they soften. Add the garlic and celery and sauté for another 3 or 4 minutes. Add the meat, breaking it up with a wooden spoon, and brown it lightly over high heat, stirring constantly.

3. Mix the tomatoes into the meat mixture and cook for 5 minutes more. Remove from the heat and pour off all but ½ cup of the liquid.

4. Sprinkle the flour over the meat and add salt and pepper to taste, the Bovril, thyme, Worcestershire sauce, bay leaf, parsley, and cilantro. Blend the meat mixture well with your hands and place it in a large casserole, patting it flat with a spoon. Leave *at least* 2 inches on top for the potatoes.

5. Boil the potatoes and remaining half onion in water to cover until tender, drain, and purée in a food mill. (Or sieve them by hand; do not use a food processor for this.) In a saucepan, melt the remaining 2 tablespoons of butter, add the milk, bring to a boil, and whisk the mixture into the puréed potatoes with ¼ cup of the Parmesan. When thoroughly blended, spread the potato mixture over the meat and sprinkle the remaining Parmesan on top of the potatoes. Bake the casserole, uncovered, for 1 hour.

BOBOTIE

In Tangier I came to know a South African writer named Noel Mostert who lived on half a shoestring but executed impressive dinner parties for the literary society of Tangier. An invitation to Noel's, in a city without a notable restaurant, meant a great deal to those of us with gastronomic concerns. The following dish, of Malay origin, derives from Noel's basic curry recipe. We've used raw lamb in place of the leftover ground meat, on which Noel relied. [D.H.]

—— SERVES 4–6 ——

3 tablespoons butter

2 pounds lean ground lamb

3 medium onions, chopped

3 cardamom pods, seeds only

¼ teaspoon ground cinnamon

⅛ teaspoon ground cloves

1 teaspoon paprika

¼ teaspoon cayenne pepper

½ teaspoon freshly ground black pepper

½ teaspoon ground ginger

1 teaspoon ground cumin

½ teaspoon ground coriander

1 teaspoon turmeric

1 teaspoon salt

1 tablespoon red wine vinegar

2 slices of coarse white bread, crusts removed

1 cup milk

2 ounces whole almonds, chopped

¼ cup raisins

¼ cup apricot preserves

3 eggs

2 tablespoons sliced blanched almonds

¼ teaspoon freshly grated nutmeg

1. Preheat the oven to 325°F.

2. In a large skillet, melt the butter and cook the meat until it's no longer pink. Transfer the meat to a bowl and drain all but 2 tablespoons of the fat. Sauté the onions over medium heat until they are golden brown. Add the spices and vinegar and continue to cook for another 3 minutes.

3. Meanwhile, soak the slices of white bread in ¼ cup of the milk for 3 minutes and then squeeze out the excess milk.

4. Add the meat and bread to the onion/spice mixture and mix with a fork until the meat is broken up. Add the chopped almonds, raisins, 2 tablespoons of the apricot preserves, and 1 egg and mix thoroughly.

5. Place the meat in a casserole large enough to leave about 2 inches on the top, smoothing the surface with a spatula. Spread the remaining 2 tablespoons of apricot preserves in a thin layer over the top.

6. In a small bowl, whisk together the remaining ¾ cup milk and 2 eggs. Pour this mixture over the layer of apricot preserves, and sprinkle with a layer of sliced almonds and the nutmeg.

7. Bake the casserole for 1 hour.

KEEMA WITH PEAS

Keema is the Indian equivalent of ground meat, but while we in America often turn it into bland formations called hamburgers, the Indians have found a way of elevating this modest fare to a more noble offering.

— SERVES 6-8 —

2 tablespoons vegetable oil

1 bay leaf

1 cinnamon stick

5 cloves

2 medium onions, chopped

3 cloves garlic, finely chopped

1 tablespoon fresh ginger, minced

1 teaspoon turmeric

1 teaspoon paprika

1 teaspoon ground coriander

2 teaspoons ground cumin

½ teaspoon cayenne pepper

½ teaspoon freshly grated nutmeg

1 cup plain yogurt

1½ cups canned Italian tomatoes, drained, seeded, and chopped

5 scallions, with ½ inch of green, sliced

1 pound ground lamb

1 pound ground beef

Salt and freshly ground pepper

2 cups fresh peas (or 1 12-ounce package frozen peas, defrosted)

Garnish: chopped fresh parsley

1. In a large casserole, heat the oil, add the bay leaf, cinnamon stick, and cloves, and cook over medium-high heat for 5 minutes, stirring constantly. Add the onions, garlic, and ginger and cook until the onions turn dark brown, 25 to 30 minutes, stirring constantly to prevent burning.

2. Add the turmeric, paprika, coriander, cumin, cayenne, and nutmeg and cook for 3 minutes, stirring constantly. Add the yogurt, 1 tablespoon at a time, mixing it in well before adding the next tablespoon.

3. Mix in the tomatoes, breaking them up with a wooden spoon, and the scallions. Add the lamb and beef and mix in well, breaking up any clumps. Cook the meat over high heat for 5 minutes. Cover, lower the heat, and simmer over low heat for 1 hour, stirring occasionally to prevent the meat from sticking. Add salt and pepper to taste. Add the fresh peas for the last 10 minutes of cooking. (If you're using frozen peas, add for the last 3 minutes, to heat through.)

4. Remove the bay leaf, cinnamon stick, and cloves, and garnish with the chopped fresh parsley.

MOUSSAKA

In this classic Greek dish, the traditional marriage of lamb and eggplant is highlighted by a suggestion of cinnamon, and, following an idea of Paula Wolfert's, topped with a yogurt sauce instead of the conventional cream sauce. Moussaka is as delicious at room temperature as it is warm. We usually serve it after a first course of Cold Avgolemono Soup (page 11), accompanied by Aromatic Rice (page 280), and followed by a simple dessert of dried fruits and nuts. This dish is better when prepared a day ahead of serving. Refrigerate it overnight, then bring to room temperature, reheat in the oven, let sit, and serve.

— SERVES 8 —

3 large eggplants, unpeeled, cut into ½-inch slices

Olive oil

3 large onions, finely chopped

3 pounds ground lamb shoulder

3 tablespoons tomato paste

¾ cup dry red wine

2 tomatoes, peeled, seeded, and chopped

¾ cup chopped fresh parsley

1 teaspoon cinnamon

Salt and freshly ground pepper

3 cups plain yogurt

4 eggs, lightly beaten

2 cups freshly grated Parmesan

¼ teaspoon freshly grated nutmeg

½ cup bread crumbs

1 tablespoon butter

1. Sprinkle the eggplant slices with salt and let them drain for 1 hour. Rinse quickly and pat dry with paper towels.

2. In a heavy skillet, heat 5 tablespoons of olive oil over medium-high heat and sauté the eggplant in batches until lightly browned on each side. Add more oil as necessary. Drain the eggplant slices on paper towels.

3. Heat 4 tablespoons of oil in the same skillet, add the onions, and sauté over medium-low heat until soft. Add the meat, raise the heat to medium, and cook, breaking up any lumps, until the meat loses its red color.

4. Preheat the oven to 375°F.

5. Dissolve the tomato paste in the wine. Add this mixture and the tomatoes, parsley, and cinnamon to the meat and cook over medium-high heat until the liquid evaporates, about 15 minutes. Add salt and pepper to taste.

6. In a small bowl, beat the yogurt and combine it with the eggs. Add 1 cup of the Parmesan and the nutmeg. Season with salt.

7. Oil an enameled or pottery baking dish, 11 by 16 inches, and sprinkle with the bread crumbs. Arrange about half the eggplant over the crumbs, overlapping the slices slightly. Sprinkle with ⅓ cup of the Parmesan. Spread all the meat mixture on top of the eggplant. Sprinkle with ⅓ cup of the Parmesan. Layer the remaining eggplant over the meat. Sprinkle with the remaining ⅓ cup of Parmesan. Pour the yogurt mixture over the top, spreading to cover completely, and dot with the butter.

8. Bake for about 45 minutes, or until the top is browned. Remove from the oven and let the moussaka stand for 15 minutes before serving.

EGGPLANT AND GROUND LAMB IN YOGURT

We sampled this Middle Eastern dish, in a slightly different form, at the old Tripoli restaurant in Brooklyn, which burned down in 1981. Serve it with a bowl of Aromatic Rice (page 280), Tabbouleh (page 271), and some warm pita bread.

—— SERVES 4-6 ——

4 cups plain yogurt

3 tablespoons butter

½ cup pine nuts

1 pound lean ground lamb

3 cloves garlic, minced

¼ cup finely chopped fresh mint

Salt and freshly ground pepper

1 large eggplant, peeled and cut into ½-inch slices

1 tablespoon olive oil

1 tablespoon cornstarch, dissolved in ¼ cup milk

1. Preheat the oven to 400°F.

2. Place the yogurt in a sieve lined with several layers of cheesecloth, drain for 15 minutes, and remove to a large casserole.

3. Melt 1 tablespoon of the butter in a small skillet and lightly brown the pine nuts. This should take 3 or 4 minutes. Drain on paper towels.

4. In a heavy skillet, melt the remaining 2 tablespoons of butter and over medium-high heat cook the lamb, mixing it with a spoon, until it is completely broken up and evenly browned, about 5 minutes. Pour off the fat and return to the heat. Add the garlic, cook for 1 more minute, and remove from the heat. Mix in the mint and add salt and pepper to taste.

5. Brush the eggplant slices lightly on both sides with the olive oil and season with salt and pepper to taste. Place the slices on a cookie sheet and bake for 8 minutes on the first side and 4 or 5 minutes on the reverse side, or until the eggplant is tender when pricked with a fork.

6. While the eggplant is cooking, add the diluted cornstarch to the yogurt and stir the yogurt with a *wooden* spoon until it becomes liquified. Slowly bring the yogurt to a simmer, stirring constantly, and in *one direction only*—this is important to keep the yogurt from separating. Remove from the heat.

7. To assemble: The lamb and yogurt should be reheated if they have cooled. On each of the warmed plates, place 2 or 3 eggplant slices and a mound of lamb removed from the skillet with a slotted spoon. Cover with yogurt and finish with a sprinkling of the toasted pine nuts.

LAMB TAGINE WITH LEMONS AND OLIVES

If this dish sounds somewhat exotic, it is. It is the first Moroccan dish I tasted upon arriving in Tangier in 1968, and one I consume at least three or four times a year. Paula Wolfert, who recorded this recipe, tells us that this tagine is one of the "great classic Moroccan specialties, spicy with a thick lemony sauce and a perfect blending of many flavors. The best olives . . . are the green-ripe olives of Morocco, which are flavored with cedrat, *a kind of thick-skinned and very fragrant lemon that grows throughout the Mediterranean region. However, you can use Greek Royal-Victorias or Kalamatas or Italian Gaetas or even California green-ripe olives marinated in a little lemon juice." [D.H.]*

—— SERVES 4-6 ——

3 pounds boneless lamb shoulder, cut into 1½-inch chunks

Pinch saffron

¼ teaspoon turmeric

1 teaspoon ground ginger

1 teaspoon paprika

½ teaspoon freshly ground black pepper

¼ teaspoon ground cumin

Salt

¼ cup vegetable oil

½ cup grated onion

¼ cup finely chopped mixed fresh herbs (parsley and cilantro)

1 large onion, minced

1 cup green-ripe olives, or "red-brown" olives

2 preserved lemons,* quartered and rinsed

Juice of 1 lemon

---

* Authentic preserved lemons require a ripening period of 30 days. The following is a shortcut version suggested by Ms. Wolfert. With a razor blade, make 8 fine 2-inch vertical incisions around the peel of each lemon to be used. (Do not cut deeper than the membrane that protects the pulp.) Place the incised lemons in a stainless steel saucepan with plenty of salt and water to cover and boil until the peels become very soft, about 5 minutes. Place in a clean jar, cover with the cooled cooking liquor, and leave to pickle for approximately 5 days.

1. Trim the lamb of excess fat. Soak the saffron in a little hot water in the bottom of a casserole. Add the spices, salt to taste, oil, and grated onion, then toss the pieces of lamb in the mixture. Sauté very gently to release the spices' aromas and *lightly* sear the meat. Add 1 cup of water and bring to a boil. Cover and simmer over low heat for 1 hour, adding water whenever necessary to avoid scorching the meat.

2. After 1 hour, add the herbs and the minced onion. Cover and simmer until the meat is very tender and the sauce is thick, about another hour and a half.

3. While the lamb is cooking, rinse and pit the olives. Remove and discard the pulp from the preserved lemons, if desired, then rinse the peels and set aside. (We julienne the lemon peels.)

4. Add the lemon juice, olives, and lemon peels 10 minutes before serving. Transfer the meat with a slotted spoon to a deep serving dish and keep warm. Reduce the sauce to about 1½ cups by boiling rapidly, uncovered, and taste for seasoning. Spoon the sauce over the lamb, decorate with the lemon peels and olives, and serve at once.

LAMB STEW WITH EGGPLANT, SAFFRON, AND GINGER

— SERVES 6 —

3 tablespoons butter

2 tablespoons olive oil

3 pounds boneless lamb shoulder, cut into 1½-inch cubes

1 tablespoon sugar

¼ cup flour

Salt and freshly ground pepper

2 medium onions, chopped

2 cloves garlic, finely chopped

¼ teaspoon saffron

2 carrots, cut in half lengthwise and then into ¼-inch slices

3 tomatoes, peeled, seeded, and chopped

1 medium potato, peeled and chopped

1 small eggplant, peeled and cubed

1 cup dry red wine

¼ teaspoon cinnamon

½ teaspoon turmeric

1 teaspoon ground ginger

¼ teaspoon freshly grated nutmeg

1 teaspoon paprika

1 teaspoon ground cumin

1½ cups Chicken Stock* (page 5)

½ cup chopped fresh parsley

Garnish: chopped fresh parsley or cilantro

---

* For added richness and flavor, add a few lamb bones when you prepare the chicken stock. If your stock is already made, this can be done by letting the bones simmer in the stock for an hour or two, straining the liquid through a sieve lined with several layers of cheesecloth, and skimming off the fat that rises to the surface.

1. Preheat the oven to 500°F.

2. In a large skillet, melt 1 tablespoon of the butter with the oil. Add the pieces of lamb, a few at a time, and brown on all sides over medium-high heat, transferring them to a large flameproof casserole as they are done. Sprinkle the lamb in the casserole with the sugar and stir over high heat for 3 or 4 minutes, until the sugar has caramelized. Add the flour and salt and pepper to taste and mix thoroughly. Bake, uncovered, for 8 minutes, stirring once after 4 minutes. Remove the casserole from the oven and set aside. Reduce the oven temperature to 325°F.

3. Melt the remaining 2 tablespoons of butter in the skillet in which the meat was browned. Add the onions, garlic, and saffron and sauté over medium heat until the onions are soft, mixing well so the saffron is evenly distributed. Add the carrots, tomatoes, potato, and eggplant and cook until the vegetables soften a bit. Add this mixture to the casserole.

4. Pour the wine into the skillet and over medium heat scrape up the bits clinging to the bottom. Pour this into the casserole and add the cinnamon, turmeric, ginger, nutmeg, ½ teaspoon pepper, paprika, and cumin. Mix and cook over medium heat for a few minutes to distribute the spices and release their flavors.

5. Add the stock and mix thoroughly. (The stew can be made up to this point and set aside until you're ready to prepare your meal.)

6. Bring the casserole to a simmer, then cover and bake for 1 hour. Add the parsley and bake, uncovered, for another 15 minutes to thicken the sauce.

7. Garnish with the chopped fresh parsley or cilantro.

LAMB STEW WITH ROSEMARY AND CAPERS

4½ pounds boneless lamb shoulder, cut into 1½-inch cubes, excess fat and gristle removed

¼ cup olive oil

2 medium onions, finely chopped

1 celery stalk, finely chopped

1 carrot, peeled and finely chopped

4 cloves garlic, minced

2 cups dry white wine

8 anchovy fillets, chopped

1 cup canned Italian tomatoes, drained, seeded, and chopped

2 bay leaves

1½ teaspoons dried rosemary, crushed

½ teaspoon salt

Freshly ground pepper

3 tablespoons lemon juice

2 tablespoons capers, drained and chopped

¼ cup chopped fresh parsley

1. Preheat the oven to 325°F.

2. Dry the lamb with paper towels. In a casserole that is large enough to hold all the meat, heat the oil over medium-high heat. Add the lamb and brown it on all sides in batches. Add more oil if necessary. As the meat is browned, use a slotted spoon to transfer it to a plate. Set aside.

3. Once the lamb is browned, there should be about 3 tablespoons of oil in the casserole. In it sauté the onions, celery, and carrot over medium-low heat until tender, scraping up the brown bits in the casserole. Add the garlic for the last minute of cooking.

4. Return the meat and any accumulated juices to the casserole. Add the wine, raise the heat to high, and reduce the wine for 1 minute. Add the anchovies, tomatoes, bay leaves, rosemary, salt, and pepper to taste, cover the casserole, and bake until the meat is tender, about 1½ hours. When ready to serve, gently stir in the lemon juice, capers, and chopped fresh parsley.

LAMB IN DILLED SOUR CREAM SAUCE

—— SERVES 6 ——

2 tablespoons vegetable oil

2 tablespoons butter

4 pounds boneless lamb shoulder, cut into 1½-inch cubes and trimmed

1 medium onion, finely chopped

3 cloves garlic, minced

¼ cup flour

½ cup dry white wine

½ teaspoon dill seed

1 pound fresh mushrooms, quartered

Salt and freshly ground pepper

1 cup sour cream

Grated rind of ½ lemon

¼ cup chopped fresh dill (or 1 tablespoon dried dill)

Garnish: chopped fresh dill or parsley

1. In a large flameproof casserole, heat the oil and butter and brown the lamb, removing the pieces to a plate as they are done.

2. Return the lamb and juices to the casserole, add the onion and garlic, and cook over medium heat for 3 minutes. Sprinkle with the flour and mix well. Continue cooking over medium heat for another 3 minutes.

3. Add the wine and dill seed and bring to a boil; then reduce the heat and simmer, covered, for 1 hour. Remove the fat that rises to the surface.

4. Bring the casserole to a simmer again over medium heat, add the mushrooms and salt and pepper to taste, and cook for 30 minutes. Remove from the heat and add the sour cream, lemon rind, and dill. Garnish with the chopped fresh dill or parsley.

LAMB SHANKS
WITH WHITE BEANS

1½ pounds dried white Great Northern beans

5 cloves garlic

6 lamb shanks, about 1 pound each

Flour seasoned with salt and freshly ground pepper for dredging

¼ cup olive oil

2 medium onions, chopped

1 large carrot, peeled and chopped

1 large celery stalk, chopped

1 cup canned Italian tomatoes, with liquid, chopped

1 teaspoon dried rosemary

1 teaspoon dried thyme

1 teaspoon salt

Freshly ground pepper

1 cup dry white wine

4 cups Chicken Stock (page 5)

2 bay leaves

½ cup chopped fresh parsley

1. Soak the beans overnight in cold water to cover. Drain the beans, place in a large saucepan, and add enough water to cover the beans by 2 inches. Bring to a boil, then lower the heat and simmer for 1 hour. Drain and set aside.

2. Preheat the oven to 325°F.

3. Sliver 2 of the garlic cloves. With a pointed knife, make small incisions in the lamb shanks and insert the garlic.

4. Pat the shanks dry and dredge them in the seasoned flour. Shake off the excess. Heat the oil in a large flameproof oval casserole over medium-high heat, then add the shanks and brown on all sides, working in batches. Set aside on a plate as they are done.

5. There should be about 3 tablespoons of oil left in the casserole. Reduce the heat to medium-low, add the onions, carrot, and celery, and sauté until lightly browned. Mince the remaining 3 garlic cloves and add for the last minute of cooking.

6. In a large bowl, toss the drained beans, sautéed vegetables, tomatoes and their liquid, rosemary, thyme, and salt and pepper to taste. Return the shanks and any accumulated liquid to the casserole and pour the bean mixture over the meat. Add the wine and enough stock to barely cover the beans. Add the bay leaves.

7. Bring the casserole to a simmer on top of the stove. Cover and bake until the shanks and beans are tender, about 1½ hours, checking occasionally to be sure there's enough liquid.

8. Arrange the shanks around the rim of a large heated platter. Remove the bay leaves, stir the parsley into the beans, and mound the beans in the center of the platter.

LAMB, SAUSAGE, AND WHITE BEAN STEW

A classic cassoulet takes days to prepare. This dish, a variation on a recipe in Paula Wolfert's Mediterranean Cooking, *is quicker and extremely good.*

—— SERVES 6-8 ——

1 pound dried white Great
  Northern beans

2 cups cold water

¼ pound salt pork, chopped

5 sprigs parsley

6 cloves garlic, chopped

1 medium onion, stuck with
  2 cloves

1 bay leaf

½ teaspoon dried thyme

1 tablespoon butter

1 tablespoon olive oil

Salt and freshly ground pepper

2 pounds boneless lamb
  shoulder, cut into 1½-inch
  cubes

Flour

2 medium onions, cut in half
  and thinly sliced

3 thick slices slab bacon, cut
  into ¼-inch slices

1 pound kielbasa, cut into
  ¼-inch slices

1 cup Beef Stock (page 6)

1 cup canned Italian tomatoes,
  drained, seeded, and
  chopped

½ cup dry red wine

½ cup homemade bread
  crumbs

4 tablespoons butter, melted

1. Soak the beans overnight in cold water to cover. Drain and set aside. Place the salt pork and the cold water in a saucepan, bring to a boil; then lower the heat and simmer for 5 minutes. Drain.

2. In a stockpot, combine the parsley sprigs (tie them together so they can be extracted easily later on), 3 of the garlic cloves, the onion with cloves, bay leaf, thyme, beans, salt pork, and enough water to cover the beans by 2 inches. Bring to a boil, then lower the heat and simmer, covered, until the beans are tender, about 1½ hours.

3. In a casserole, melt the butter with the oil. Season the lamb with salt and pepper and lightly dust it with the flour. Brown the lamb, a few pieces at a time, and set aside.

4. Add a little oil to the casserole if necessary, then sauté the sliced onions and bacon over medium heat, until the onions have softened. Return the lamb to the casserole with the remaining garlic, the kielbasa, stock, tomatoes, and wine and simmer, partially covered, for 1 hour. After about 45 minutes, preheat the oven to 300°F.

5. Drain the beans and salt pork over a bowl, discarding the parsley, onion, and bay leaf and reserving 1 cup of the liquid. When the meat has cooked for 1 hour, add the reserved liquid, beans, and salt pork to the casserole and mix well. Sprinkle a layer of the bread crumbs over the top, drizzle the melted butter over them, and bake, uncovered, for 1½ hours.

BIGOS

Bigos is a Polish invention, a hunter's stew, that can be made with various meats—pheasant, venison, boar—whatever has been caught. Some say it is the national dish of Poland. The recipe that follows is rather tame, in that it calls for lamb, beef, and pork. Feel free to substitute, to experiment, to hunt.

—— SERVES 8 ——

1 ounce dried porcini mushrooms

2 pounds sauerkraut, rinsed well and drained

½ head small cabbage, finely shredded

4 tomatoes, peeled, seeded, and chopped

1 pound kielbasa, cut into 1-inch slices

6 tablespoons butter

¼ pound slab bacon, cut into thin slices

1 large onion, cut in half and thinly sliced

1 green cooking apple, peeled, cored, and chopped

3 cloves garlic, chopped

1 pound fresh mushrooms, cut in half

3 tablespoons olive oil

1 pound boneless pork shoulder or butt, cut into 1½-inch cubes

1 pound boneless lamb shoulder, cut into 1½-inch pieces

1 pound beef chuck, cut into 1½-inch pieces

¼ cup dry sherry

½ teaspoon paprika

Salt and freshly ground pepper

2 cups Beef Stock (page 6)

1 cup dry red wine

1 cup sour cream, at room temperature

1. Cover the dried mushrooms with hot water and let soak for 1 hour. Remove the mushrooms from the liquid, chop them, and place in a large mixing bowl. Strain the liquid through a sieve lined with several layers of cheesecloth and reserve.

2. Preheat the oven to 325°F.

3. Add the sauerkraut, cabbage, tomatoes, and kielbasa to the mixing bowl.

4. In a large casserole, heat 3 tablespoons of the butter, add the bacon, and cook over low heat until the fat has been rendered. With a slotted spoon, transfer the bacon to the mixing bowl.

5. Add the onion, apple, and garlic to the rendered fat in the casserole, and cook over medium heat for 3 minutes. Mix in the fresh and soaked dried mushrooms and cook for another 3 minutes, stirring to prevent them from burning. Add this mixture to the mixing bowl.

6. Add the remaining 3 tablespoons of butter and the oil to the casserole and in it brown the meat over high heat in batches, removing it to the mixing bowl as it is done.

7. When the last of the meat is browned, add the sherry and reserved mushroom liquid. Reduce this liquid over high heat for 1 minute, scraping up the bits clinging to the bottom of the casserole, and pour it over the meat in the mixing bowl. Stir in the paprika, add salt and pepper to taste, and combine thoroughly.

8. Return the contents of the mixing bowl to the casserole, add the stock and wine, cover, and bake for 1½ hours. Remove the cover, stir, and bake for 30 minutes more. Remove the casserole from the oven, whisk a little of the cooking liquid into the sour cream, then carefully fold the diluted sour cream into the stew, combining thoroughly.

POZOLE

Friends of ours from New Mexico suggested we include a recipe for this Mexican/New Mexican favorite. The recipe that follows is a variation on one sent to us by the Catrons of Santa Fe. It is a heavy soup/stew, enriched with hominy and pork bones. A serious and picante winter stew.

—— SERVES 8 ——

5 dried chilies (a combination of ancho, pasilla, and serranos, if possible)

2 cups boiling water

2 pounds pork loin, cut into 1½-inch pieces

¼ pound pork rinds (*queritos*), cut into strips

One 4-pound chicken, cut into serving pieces

4 cloves garlic, chopped

5 cups Chicken Stock (page 5)

2 pounds pork bones

3 pig's feet

3 medium onions, sliced

1 bay leaf

2 sprigs fresh oregano (or ½ teaspoon dried oregano)

4 cups canned whole hominy, drained

Salt

GARNISH

¼ cup finely chopped cilantro

½ head iceberg lettuce, chopped

1 large onion, finely chopped

8 wedges lime

1 dish mixed spices (5 tablespoons ground cumin, 5 tablespoons dried oregano, 2 tablespoons chili powder)

2 avocados, sliced

Fresh hot tortillas

1. Cover the chilies with the boiling water, let them stand for 1 hour, and drain, reserving the liquid. Remove the stems, seeds, and inside veins (it's best to wear plastic gloves when you do this) and purée the chilies in a food processor with the reserved water.

2. In a large glass or ceramic bowl, place the pork, pork rinds, chicken, garlic, chili purée, and the stock. Cover and refrigerate overnight.

3. Drain the liquid from the meat mixture into a large casserole and reserve the meat. To the liquid, add the pork bones, pig's feet, 1 of the onions, the bay leaf, and oregano. Bring to a boil and simmer, covered, for 3 hours, occasionally skimming the scum that rises to the surface.

4. Strain the sauce through a fine sieve, pressing down on the solids to extract as much liquid as possible. Discard the solids, skim off the fat that rises to the surface, and return the sauce to the casserole.

5. Add the remaining 2 onions, the reserved meat, except for the chicken pieces, and the hominy and simmer for 1 hour. Add the chicken (and any juices that have accumulated) and simmer for another 30 minutes, or until the chicken is tender. Add salt to taste.

6. Serve in large bowls with a bit of the cilantro scattered over the top of each bowl and the other garnishes on individual plates placed around the table.

BLACK BEAN AND FOUR-SAUSAGE CASSEROLE

If you're like us, always searching for the sausage in bean dishes such as feijoada and cassoulet, this recipe is for you. With only sausage, search and seizure will not be necessary.

— SERVES 8 —

1 pound dried black beans

½ pound salt pork, cut into 1-inch pieces

BOUQUET GARNI

1 carrot, quartered

10 sprigs parsley

1 bay leaf

1 celery stalk with leaves, quartered

2 sprigs fresh thyme (or 1 teaspoon dried thyme)

1 dried red chili pepper (optional)

1 medium onion, stuck with 2 cloves

3 cloves garlic, lightly crushed

2 pounds kielbasa, cut into ¾-inch slices

2 tablespoons olive oil

6 hot Italian sausages

2 linguica or chorizo sausages

2 bockwurst (veal and pork sausage)

2 cups dry red wine

1½ cups canned Italian tomatoes, drained, seeded, and chopped

Salt and freshly ground pepper

½ cup chopped cilantro or fresh parsley

1. Soak the beans overnight in water to cover. Drain the beans and place them in a large casserole with the salt pork, bouquet garni, and the kielbasa. Add enough cold water to cover the mixture by 2 inches, bring to a boil, lower the heat, and simmer for 1 hour.

2. Preheat the oven to 200°F.

3. In a large skillet, heat the oil over medium-high heat and in it brown the Italian sausages, the linguica, and the bockwurst, pricking them with a fork.

4. Remove the bouquet garni and discard. Drain the beans, salt pork, and kielbasa mixture through a sieve set over a bowl and return them to the casserole, reserving the liquid. Add the wine, tomatoes, and salt and pepper to taste. Slice the Italian sausages, the linguica, and the bockwurst into pieces, add to the beans with enough of the reserved bean liquid to just cover the mixture, and cover the casserole. Bake for 2 hours, stirring every 20 minutes or so. If the beans get too dry, add a little of the remaining bean liquid.

5. Mix in the chopped cilantro or fresh parsley and serve.

COTECHINO AND LENTILS

Cotechino is a marvelous-tasting Italian sausage that is available at Italian butchers. If you can't find it, you could substitute Italian sweet sausage or Polish kielbasa (simmered in a skillet in an inch of water, pricked, and browned when the water has evaporated).

— SERVES 6 —

1 cotechino, about 1½ pounds

8 tablespoons olive oil

1 large onion, chopped

1 celery stalk, chopped

1 carrot, peeled and chopped

3 cloves garlic, minced

1 pound lentils, rinsed and drained

1½ cups canned Italian tomatoes, drained, seeded, and chopped

5 cups Chicken Stock (page 5)

2 bay leaves

1 teaspoon dried thyme

½ teaspoon fennel seeds, crushed

½ cup chopped fresh parsley

Salt and freshly ground pepper

1. In a large saucepan, cover the *cotechino* with cold water, bring to a boil, reduce the heat, and simmer for 2 hours. Turn off the heat and leave the *cotechino* in its cooking liquid. When the *cotechino* has cooked for 1 hour, start preparing the lentils.

2. In a casserole, heat the olive oil, add the onion, celery, and carrot, and cook over medium-low heat until tender. Add the garlic for the last minute of cooking.

3. Add the lentils and stir to coat with oil. Add the tomatoes, stock, bay leaves, thyme, and fennel. Bring to a boil, then lower the heat and simmer very slowly, covered, until the lentils are tender, 45 minutes to 1 hour. Remove the bay leaves and stir in the parsley. Add salt and pepper to taste.

4. Remove the *cotechino* from its cooking liquid and cut into ½-inch slices. Put the lentils in a warm serving bowl and lay the *cotechino* slices over them.

HAM HOCKS AND LIMA BEANS

— SERVES 6 —

1 pound dried baby lima beans

One 28-ounce can Italian
tomatoes

2 tablespoons Dijon mustard

2 tablespoons dark brown
sugar

¼ cup bacon fat or oil

1 large onion, chopped

1 celery stalk, chopped

1 green bell pepper, seeded
and chopped

3 cloves garlic, minced

¼ teaspoon cayenne pepper

½ teaspoon dried thyme

½ teaspoon dried marjoram

6 smoked ham hocks

5 cups Chicken Stock (page 5)

2 bay leaves

Salt and freshly ground pepper

1. Soak the beans overnight in cold water. Drain the beans and set aside.

2. Preheat the oven to 325°F.

3. Drain the tomatoes and reserve the liquid. Seed and chop the tomatoes and set aside. Dissolve the mustard and brown sugar in the tomato liquid and set aside.

4. In a large casserole, heat the bacon fat or oil over medium-low heat. Add the onion, celery, and pepper and sauté until soft. Add the garlic for the last minute of cooking.

5. Add the tomatoes, tomato liquid, cayenne, thyme, marjoram, beans, ham hocks, and enough stock to barely cover the beans and hocks. Add the bay leaves and salt and pepper to taste.

6. Bring the mixture to a simmer, then cover and bake until the beans and hocks are tender, about 1½ to 2 hours, checking occasionally to be sure there is enough liquid.

7. Remove the bay leaves. Spoon the beans onto a heated serving dish, arrange the hocks on the beans, and serve.

CHOUCROUTE GARNIE

We first cooked a choucroute garnie *with friends who had spent much time in the Alsace region, and who promised us that this dish transformed the humble sauerkraut into a marvel of subtlety. We've trusted their taste ever since. On that first go-round, we used their homemade sausages, which were incomparable, but bratwurst from a good German butcher come close. The goose fat makes for a richer, more unctuous dish, but if you can't find it, don't deny yourself the pleasure of a* choucroute. *It should be served with a Riesling, Gewürztraminer, or a dark German beer.*

— SERVES 8 —

3 pounds sauerkraut (preferably bagged or jarred)

½ pound slab bacon (preferably double-smoked), cut into ½-inch dice

2 large onions, chopped

4 cloves garlic, minced

2 green apples, peeled, cored, and finely chopped

½ teaspoon dried thyme

2 bay leaves

1 tablespoon juniper berries, bruised

1 teaspoon peppercorns, bruised

2 cups dry white wine

4 cups Chicken Stock (page 5)

¼ cup goose fat (available in tins at specialty shops)

16 small new potatoes

8 bratwurst or 2 pounds kielbasa, cut into 4-inch lengths

8 smoked pork chops

Garnish: chopped fresh parsley

1. Drain the sauerkraut in a colander and rinse under cold running water. Place in a large bowl of cold water and soak for 30 minutes. Drain in a colander and squeeze by the handful to remove excess liquid. Set aside.

2. In a large casserole, sauté the bacon over medium-low heat, stirring occasionally, until it has browned and rendered most of its fat. Add the onions and sauté until tender. Add the garlic for the last minute of cooking.

3. Add the sauerkraut, apples, thyme, bay leaves, juniper berries, peppercorns, wine, and stock. Spoon the goose fat over the top. Bring to a simmer, lay a buttered round of waxed paper over the top, cover, and cook at the slightest simmer for 4 hours.

4. Add the new potatoes, pushing them down into the sauerkraut, and cook for 1 hour more.

5. Meanwhile, place the bratwurst or kielbasa in a skillet with ½ cup of water. Bring the water to a boil and cook, turning the sausages a couple of times and pricking them with a fork. When the water has evaporated, brown the sausages in the fat that remains in the skillet. Set aside. Brown the pork chops quickly in the sausage fat over medium-high heat and set aside.

6. When the potatoes have cooked for 1 hour, or are nearly tender, add the sausages and pork chops to the casserole, pressing them into the sauerkraut. Cook for another 30 minutes.

7. Place the sausages, pork chops, and potatoes around the edge of a heated serving platter. Heap the sauerkraut in the middle and garnish with the chopped fresh parsley.

GOULASH

You may substitute veal—shoulder or rump—
for pork in this recipe. Pork is considerably cheaper and,
we think, better.

—— SERVES 8 ——

3 tablespoons lard or
cooking oil

4 pounds boneless pork
shoulder, cut into 1½-inch
cubes, trimmed of fat

4 large onions, sliced

3 tablespoons sweet
Hungarian paprika

3 cloves garlic, minced

2 tablespoons tomato paste

1 teaspoon salt

2 tablespoons flour

2 cups Chicken Stock (page 5)

1 bay leaf

2 bell peppers, green or red,
seeded, cut in half and
sliced into ¼-inch strips

2 teaspoons caraway seeds,
crushed

1 cup sour cream, at room
temperature

2 tablespoons Dijon mustard

1. Preheat the oven to 350°F.

2. In a heavy casserole, heat the lard or oil over medium-high heat and sauté the pork quickly in batches, to seal it. Set it aside on a plate as it is done.

3. After the pork is seared, there should be about 3 tablespoons of fat in the casserole. Reduce the heat to medium-low and sauté the onions until soft, scraping up the brown bits on the bottom of the casserole.

4. Return the meat and any accumulated juices to the casserole. Raise the heat to medium and stir in the paprika. Cook for 2 to 3 minutes, add the garlic, tomato paste, and salt, and cook for a few minutes. Sprinkle in the flour, toss, and cook for a few minutes more, stirring.

5. In a saucepan, bring the stock to a boil and add it with the bay leaf to the casserole. Bring to a boil again, cover, and bake for 45 minutes.

6. Stir the peppers into the casserole, return to the oven, and bake for another 30 minutes.

7. Stir the crushed caraway seeds into the casserole, return to the oven, and bake until the meat is tender, about 15 minutes. Remove from the oven. (*Note:* You may prepare this ahead of time through Step 7, that is, when you remove the goulash from the oven. About 15 minutes before you plan to serve it, bring the casserole to a strong simmer on top of the stove and proceed with Step 8.)

8. When the goulash is done, remove the bay leaf. Skim any fat from the surface of the stew. Beat the sour cream and mustard with a whisk, then beat in ½ cup of the cooking liquid to thin it. Add the sour cream mixture to the casserole, carefully folding it into the goulash.

PORK STEW WITH DRIED MUSHROOMS AND JUNIPER BERRIES

A recipe inspired by Marcella Hazan.

—— SERVES 8 ——

- 2 ounces dried porcini mushrooms
- 1 cup hot water
- ⅓ cup olive oil
- 4 pounds boneless pork shoulder or butt, cut into 1½-inch cubes, fat removed
- 1 medium onion, finely chopped
- 2 leeks, white part only, cleaned, cut in half lengthwise and then into thin strips
- 2 cloves garlic, minced
- 2 teaspoons tomato paste
- 2 cups dry white wine
- 3 tablespoons white wine vinegar
- 1 teaspoon salt
- Freshly ground pepper
- 1 teaspoon dried thyme
- 2 bay leaves
- 8 anchovy fillets, chopped
- 1 heaping tablespoon juniper berries, bruised

1. Soak the mushrooms in the hot water for 1 hour. Remove the mushrooms from the liquid, chop, and set aside. Drain the liquid through a sieve lined with several layers of cheesecloth and set aside.

2. Preheat the oven to 325°F.

3. Pat the pork dry. In a heavy casserole large enough to hold all the meat, heat the oil over medium-high heat. Add the pork and brown it quickly in batches, removing it with a slotted spoon to a plate when browned.

4. Reduce the heat to medium-low, add the onion and leeks, and sauté until soft, scraping up the bits of meat at the bottom of the casserole. Add the garlic for the last minute of cooking.

5. Return the pork and any accumulated juices to the casserole. Dissolve the tomato paste in the wine and add the vinegar; pour this mixture into the casserole. Add the salt and pepper to taste, raise the heat, and boil the liquid for 2 or 3 minutes.

6. Add the mushrooms and their liquid, the thyme, bay leaves, anchovies, and juniper berries. Stir to distribute evenly. Cover and bake until the meat is tender, about 1½ hours, basting occasionally.

7. Transfer the meat to a heated platter. Check the sauce for salt and pepper, and pour it over the meat. Serve immediately.

WINTER PORK AND FRUIT RAGOUT

The cohabitation of fruit and meat is something we favor, and this stew makes the most of that marriage. We usually add 36 whole blanched almonds, toasted in the oven for 15 minutes and scattered over the finished dish. This recipe comes from The Silver Palate Cookbook *by Julee Rosso and Sheila Lukins.*

—— SERVES 6–8 ——

3 pounds lean boneless pork, cut into 1-inch cubes

2 dozen dried apricot halves

1 cup dark seedless raisins

1 cup dry red wine

1 cup red wine vinegar

3 tablespoons chopped fresh dill

3 tablespoons chopped fresh mint

1 teaspoon ground cumin seeds

1 teaspoon freshly ground black pepper

1 tablespoon dried thyme

Salt

⅓ cup olive oil

4 shallots, peeled and minced

1 cup dry white wine

4 cups Chicken Stock (page 5)

2 bay leaves

¼ cup honey

1. In a large bowl, combine the pork, apricots, raisins, red wine, vinegar, dill, mint, cumin seeds, pepper, thyme, and salt to taste. Cover and marinate, refrigerated, for 24 hours. Stir occasionally.

2. Preheat the oven to 350°F. Position a rack in the middle of the oven.

3. Remove the pork and fruit from the marinade, reserving the fruit and the marinade separately. Pat the pork dry with paper towels.

4. Heat the olive oil in a large skillet and sauté the meat, a few pieces at a time, until well browned. With a slotted spoon, transfer the pork to a deep casserole.

5. Drain the oil from the skillet, add the shallots, and sauté over medium heat for 5 minutes. Add the reserved marinade and bring to a boil, scraping up any browned bits remaining in the skillet. Cook for several minutes, until slightly reduced, and add to the casserole.

6. Stir in the fruit, half of the white wine, half of the chicken stock, the bay leaves, and honey; mix well. Bring to a boil over medium heat; then cover and bake for 1 hour and 15 minutes. Uncover the casserole and add more wine or stock if the meat seems too dry. Bake, uncovered, for another 30 to 45 minutes, or until the meat is tender and the sauce rich and thick.

PASTAS

It is common knowledge that the Italians take their pasta with considerably more than a grain of salt. It has been claimed that it was Savonarola, the gravedigger of Florence, who shouted from his pulpit: "It's not enough for you to eat your pasta fried. No! You think you have to add garlic to it, and when you eat ravioli, it's not enough to boil it in a pot and eat it in its own juice, you have to fry it in another pan and cover it with cheese!" The Florentines, evidently tired of such fanaticism, ended his reign by roasting him.

In putting together these pasta recipes, we decided to include risottos in this section. Although risotto is technically not a pasta, and the procedure for cooking it is different, it seems to be a very close relative in spirit. Risotto uses many of the same ingredients as pasta, and, like pasta, is traditionally served as a first course. In any case, there are few dishes more satisfying than a well-prepared risotto.

You can achieve the proper texture of a risotto only by using Italian Arborio rice; because of the way risotto is cooked, long-grain rice cannot be substituted. Our directions for cooking risotto are simple but should be followed carefully. The most important thing to keep in mind is that the liquid must be added gradually—risotto is not boiled rice.

As noted in the Ingredients section, if you choose not to make your own pasta and fresh pasta is not readily available in your neighborhood, boxed pasta may be used, but only those pastas imported from Italy. All pasta should be cooked al dente—firm to the bite but not crunchy.

Fresh pasta will need only 10 to 30 seconds of cooking after the water returns to a boil; keep a close watch on it. Boxed pasta will take 10 to 15 minutes, depending on the shape of the pasta. Stir it with a wooden spoon after you've dropped it into the boiling water to prevent it from sticking together. Ideally, the sauce and pasta should be finished simultaneously, but as the world is not perfect, this cannot always be arranged. It is essential, however, that the pasta not be ready before the sauce, and most sauces do not suffer from being gently reheated. If you are using fresh pasta, your sauce should be finished before you put the pasta into the boiling water; if you are using boxed pasta, there is usually time to finish most sauces while the pasta is cooking.

Although pasta shapes are *sometimes* interchangeable, we have suggested shapes that complement the sauces they are served with. For example, fusilli is an excellent shape for trapping small bits of an ingredient in a sauce and thereby dispersing them throughout the dish, as in Fusilli with Red Caviar, Fennel, and Cream. Lasagne, obviously, is structurally necessary to the dishes in which it is used. And some shapes are traditionally associated with particular sauces, such as in Linguine with White Clam Sauce, Fettuccine with Cream, Parmesan, and Parsley, and Spaghetti alla Carbonara.

Although it might seem unconventional to an Italian, we often serve pasta as a main course, preceded by a first course such as crostini or caponata, and followed by a green salad. Most pastas should be served with an accompanying bowl of freshly grated Parmesan cheese and a pepper mill. One pound of pasta will serve four comfortably as a main course, and six as a first course. Very rich pastas—Spaghettini with Walnuts and Marjoram, for example, or Linguine with Gorgonzola Sauce—are best served as a first course, as are risottos. Despite claims to the contrary, you can sometimes have too much of a good thing.

FRESH PASTA

The following recipe for making your own fresh egg pasta is not difficult, but it takes some practice and patience to get the hang of it. We have written it for those who wish to do it entirely by hand, as well as for those who own a pasta machine.

—— MAKES ABOUT 1 POUND OF PASTA ——

2½ cups all-purpose flour

3 eggs, at room temperature, lightly beaten with a fork

1 teaspoon salt

2 teaspoons olive oil

Lukewarm water

1. In a large bowl, place the flour. Put your fist in the middle of the mound of flour to create a well. Pour the eggs into the cavity and add the salt and oil. Using your fingers, combine the eggs and flour with a circular motion, working slowly outward, until the eggs are completely incorporated into the flour. Add water, starting with a teaspoonful, to make a stiff but still flexible dough that can be formed into a ball.

2. Knead the dough on a lightly floured wooden or marble surface, folding and pressing the dough with the heels of your hands and turning it slightly after each knead, until the dough is smooth and elastic, about 10 minutes. If the dough starts to stick, add a little more flour. Let the dough sit for 30 minutes, covered with a damp kitchen towel.

3. BY HAND. Divide the dough into 2 parts and flatten each with your hand. Roll each half out on a floured surface, turning and dusting with flour as necessary, until very thin, about ¹⁄₁₆ of an inch. The entire rolling process should take less than 10 minutes. Let the sheets dry for about 20 minutes, but do not allow them to get brittle.

BY PASTA MACHINE. (These are general instructions. It is a good idea to refer to the instructions that come with your pasta machine.) Quarter the ball of dough. Set the opening of the roller side of the machine to wide and run each quarter through, gradually reducing the setting. Pass the sheet through again and again, rolling it thinner and thinner, until it is too wide for the rollers. When you have reached this point, cut each sheet in half and proceed until you achieve the desired thickness. Let the sheets dry for 20 minutes before proceeding, but do not allow them to get brittle.

4. BY HAND. Roll each sheet up into a moderately tight flat roll and with a sharp floured knife, slice it crosswise into strips of the desired thickness. Unroll each strand and leave on a floured surface for 10 minutes or until ready to use.

BY PASTA MACHINE. Run each sheet through the cutting side of the machine and lay the pasta on a floured surface for 10 minutes, or until ready to use.

PENNE ALLA PUTTANESCA

4 cloves garlic, minced

3 tablespoons olive oil

10 anchovy fillets, chopped

3 cups canned Italian tomatoes, *not* drained

¼ pound green olives (preferably Sicilian) with pimientos, sliced

½ pound black olives (Kalamata or Gaeta), pitted and sliced

2 teaspoons capers, drained

2 tablespoons chopped fresh basil (or 2 teaspoons dried basil)

1 teaspoon red pepper flakes (or more to taste)

2 tablespoons vegetable oil

1 tablespoon salt

1 pound penne rigate (ribbed penne)

Freshly grated Parmesan

1. In a large skillet, briefly sauté the garlic in the oil over medium-low heat, without letting it color.

2. Add the anchovies and tomatoes and simmer for 5 minutes, stirring occasionally, to break up the tomatoes and prevent burning.

3. Stir in the olives, capers, basil, and red pepper flakes and simmer, uncovered, for 45 minutes, until the liquid has cooked off and the sauce has thickened.

4. In a stockpot, bring 5 quarts of water to a boil and add the salt and vegetable oil. Add the penne, stir, and cook until al dente. Drain and transfer to a large bowl. Toss with the sauce (reheated if necessary) and serve with a bowl of freshly grated Parmesan on the side.

PENNE ALL'ARRABBIATA

— SERVES 4–6 —

3 tablespoons olive oil

½ medium onion, finely chopped

2 cloves garlic, minced

2 tablespoons chopped fresh basil (or 2 teaspoons dried basil)

2 hot red peppers, finely chopped (or 2 teaspoons crushed red pepper flakes)

3 cups canned Italian tomatoes, drained, seeded, and chopped

½ cup finely chopped fresh parsley

Salt and freshly ground black pepper

2 tablespoons vegetable oil

1 pound penne rigate (ribbed penne)

Garnish: chopped fresh parsley and freshly grated Parmesan

1. In a large skillet, heat the oil over medium heat, add the onion, garlic, basil, and red peppers, and cook until the onions are just soft.

2. Add the tomatoes and parsley and cook over low heat until the sauce is reduced and thickened, about 1 hour. Add salt and black pepper to taste.

3. In a stockpot, bring 5 quarts of water to a boil and add 1 tablespoon of salt and the vegetable oil. Add the penne, stir, and cook until al dente. Drain and transfer to a large bowl. Toss with the sauce (reheated if necessary), garnish with the chopped fresh parsley, and serve with a bowl of freshly grated Parmesan on the side.

BUCATINI ALL'AMATRICIANA

For a heavier, richer sauce, cook the bacon before you prepare the tomato sauce and sauté the onion in bacon fat instead of olive oil.

— SERVES 4-6 —

¼ cup olive oil

1 medium onion, chopped

3 cloves garlic, minced

½ cup white wine

3 cups canned Italian tomatoes, drained, seeded, and chopped

1 teaspoon dried marjoram

Freshly ground pepper

½ pound sliced bacon

1 tablespoon salt

2 tablespoons vegetable oil

1 pound bucatini (thick hollow spaghetti)

½ cup freshly grated Romano cheese

Freshly grated Parmesan

1. In a saucepan, heat the oil over medium-low heat and sauté the onion until soft. Add the garlic for the last minute of cooking. Add the wine and cook at a vigorous simmer for a few minutes. Add the tomatoes, bring to a gentle simmer, and cook, covered, for 30 minutes, stirring occasionally. Add the marjoram and pepper to taste and continue cooking for another 15 minutes.

2. While the tomato sauce is cooking, in a skillet cook the bacon over low heat until all the fat is rendered but the bacon is not quite crisp. Remove and drain on paper towels. When cool, cut into ½-inch pieces and set aside.

3. In a stockpot, bring 5 quarts of water to a boil and add the salt and vegetable oil. Add the bucatini, stir, and cook until al dente. Drain thoroughly and transfer to a large bowl.

4. Toss the pasta with the tomato sauce, bacon, and Romano cheese. Served in heated bowls with a bowl of freshly grated Parmesan on the side.

SPAGHETTI WITH OLIVE OIL, GARLIC, AND PARSLEY

*As olive oil is a primary ingredient in this dish,
high-quality oil is mandatory.*

— SERVES 4–6 —

1 cup extra-virgin olive oil

4 cloves garlic, finely chopped (or more for garlic aficionados)

1 teaspoon red pepper flakes

½ cup chopped fresh parsley

Salt

2 tablespoons vegetable oil

1 pound spaghetti

Freshly grated Parmesan

1. In a large skillet, heat the oil and garlic over very low heat, stirring occasionally, to allow the garlic to turn a light, golden color as slowly as possible and to give it a chance to permeate the oil. Do not let the garlic get too brown, or it will turn bitter.

2. Remove the skillet from the heat and add the red pepper flakes, ¼ cup of the parsley, and salt to taste. Cook over low heat for 3 minutes.

3. Meanwhile, in a stockpot, bring 5 quarts of water to a boil and add 1 tablespoon of salt and the vegetable oil. Add the spaghetti, stir, and cook until not quite al dente. The pasta will cook a few minutes more in the oil. Drain the spaghetti and transfer it to the skillet. Continue to cook in the oil for another 3 minutes. Stir in the remaining parsley and serve immediately with a bowl of freshly grated Parmesan on the side.

FETTUCCINE WITH CREAM, PARMESAN, AND PARSLEY

The very simplicity of this pasta demands the best ingredients—homemade fettuccine, cooked not a second too long, and the finest Parmesan, grated just before you begin.

— SERVES 4–6 —

4 tablespoons butter

1 cup heavy cream

¾ cup freshly grated Parmesan, plus more for serving

⅛ teaspoon freshly grated nutmeg

¼ cup finely chopped fresh parsley

1 tablespoon salt

2 tablespoons vegetable oil

1 pound fettuccine

1. In a small skillet, combine 2 tablespoons of the butter and the heavy cream, bring to a gentle boil over medium heat, and cook, stirring occasionally, until the cream has thickened, about 5 minutes. Turn off the heat and stir in the Parmesan, nutmeg, and parsley.

2. With a wooden spoon, soften the remaining 2 tablespoons of butter in the bottom of a large bowl.

3. In a stockpot, bring 5 quarts of water to a boil and add the salt and vegetable oil. Add the fettuccine, stir, and cook until al dente. Drain thoroughly and add to the bowl with the butter.

4. Toss the pasta with the softened butter, add the cream sauce, and toss again. Serve in heated bowls, with additional freshly grated Parmesan.

FETTUCCINE WITH PEAS, GRATED ZEST OF LEMON, NUTMEG, AND CREAM

—— SERVES 4-6 ——

1 tablespoon salt

2 tablespoons vegetable oil

1 pound fettuccine

5 tablespoons butter

1 cup heavy cream

1 cup shelled young fresh peas, parboiled for 3 minutes (or 1 cup frozen peas, defrosted and cooked according to instructions)

Grated zest of 1 lemon (use the smallest holes on your grater)

¼ teaspoon freshly grated nutmeg

½ cup freshly grated Parmesan, plus more for serving

1. In a stockpot, bring 5 quarts of water to a boil and add the salt and vegetable oil. Add the fettuccine, stir, and cook until al dente.

2. While the pasta is cooking, in a skillet large enough to hold the pasta, heat the butter over low heat. Add the cream and the fresh peas (if you are using frozen peas, add them with the grated lemon zest in the next step) and continue to cook for 5 minutes, until the cream thickens slightly.

3. When the pasta is done, drain thoroughly and add it to the heated cream with the grated lemon zest, nutmeg, and Parmesan. Mix thoroughly and cook for 3 minutes, making sure the pasta is well coated with the sauce and the peas have heated through, but are still crisp. Serve immediately with a bowl of freshly grated Parmesan on the side.

LINGUINE WITH GORGONZOLA SAUCE

4 tablespoons butter

1 cup heavy cream

1/8 teaspoon freshly grated nutmeg

1/2 cup freshly grated Parmesan, plus more for serving

1/4 pound Gorgonzola cheese, broken into pieces

1 tablespoon salt

2 tablespoons vegetable oil

1 pound linguine

1. In a saucepan, melt the butter and add the cream, nutmeg, Parmesan, and Gorgonzola. Mix well over low heat and cook until the sauce thickens slightly, about 5 minutes.

2. In a stockpot, bring 5 quarts of water to a boil and add the salt and vegetable oil. Add the linguine, stir, and cook until al dente. Drain thoroughly.

3. Try to time the sauce so that it is ready when the pasta has finished cooking. In a large bowl, toss the linguine with the Gorgonzola sauce and serve immediately with a bowl of freshly grated Parmesan on the side.

FETTUCCINE AL PESTO WITH WALNUTS

— SERVES 4-6 —

4 cups tightly packed fresh basil leaves

3 cloves garlic, chopped

¼ cup walnuts

3 tablespoons pine nuts

2 tablespoons chopped fresh parsley

¾ cup olive oil

1 tablespoon plus 1 teaspoon salt

1 cup freshly grated Parmesan, plus more for serving

3 tablespoons softened butter

2 tablespoons vegetable oil

1 pound fettuccine

1. In a food processor, blend the basil, garlic, walnuts, pine nuts, parsley, olive oil, and 1 teaspoon of salt until smooth, scraping down the sides of the bowl to ensure an even blend.

2. Remove the pesto sauce to a bowl and stir in the Parmesan, mixing it in well. Then mix in the softened butter. (If you are going to freeze the pesto, do not add the cheese and butter at this time. When you are ready to use the pesto, let it thaw completely and proceed with the rest of the recipe, adding the cheese and butter.)

3. In a stockpot, bring 5 quarts of water to a boil and add the 1 tablespoon of salt and the vegetable oil. Add the fettuccine, stir, and cook until al dente. Drain and place in a large serving bowl. Add the pesto and toss until it is completely mixed. Serve with a bowl of freshly grated Parmesan on the side.

SPAGHETTINI WITH WALNUTS AND MARJORAM

Salt

2 tablespoons vegetable oil

1 pound spaghettini

4 tablespoons butter

1 large clove garlic, minced

½ teaspoon dried marjoram

1 cup walnuts, finely chopped

1 cup heavy cream

2 egg yolks, lightly beaten

Freshly ground pepper

½ cup freshly grated Parmesan, plus more for serving

(*Note:* If you are using dried pasta, it should be put into boiling water when you begin the sauce. If you are using fresh pasta, it should be put into boiling water after Step 2.)

1. In a stockpot, bring 5 quarts of water to a boil and add 1 tablespoon of salt and the vegetable oil. Add the spaghettini, stir, and cook until al dente. Drain thoroughly.

2. In a small skillet, heat the butter over medium heat, add the garlic and marjoram, and cook, stirring, for 2 minutes. Add the walnuts and cream, raise the heat to medium-high, and cook, stirring occasionally, until the sauce has thickened slightly, about 5 minutes. Remove from the heat and beat in the egg yolks. Add salt and pepper to taste.

3. In a bowl, toss the pasta with the sauce and the Parmesan. Serve with additional freshly grated Parmesan on the side.

LINGUINE WITH ONIONS AND CREAM

The onions for this sauce should cook very slowly until they are on the verge of becoming a purée. They must not brown.

— SERVES 6 —

4 tablespoons butter

¼ cup olive oil

4 large onions, thinly sliced

Salt

2 tablespoons vegetable oil

1 pound linguine

1 teaspoon tomato paste

½ cup heavy cream

Freshly ground pepper

½ cup freshly grated Parmesan, plus more for serving

1. In a large heavy skillet, heat the butter and oil, add the onions, and toss to coat them. Cover and cook over *very* low heat for 30 minutes, stirring occasionally. Add salt to taste, stir, and continue to cook, covered, over very low heat, stirring occasionally, for 1 more hour, or until the onions are a golden color and very soft.

2. In a stockpot, bring 5 quarts of water to a boil and add 1 tablespoon of salt and the vegetable oil. Add the linguine, stir, and cook until al dente. Drain thoroughly.

3. While the pasta is cooking—or, if you are using fresh pasta, while the water is coming to the boil—dissolve the tomato paste in the heavy cream. Add this mixture and a generous grinding of pepper to the onions. Cook over medium heat, stirring, for a few minutes, or until the cream is slightly thickened.

4. In a large bowl, toss the linguine with the onion sauce and the Parmesan. Serve with a bowl of freshly grated Parmesan on the side.

SPAGHETTI ALLA CARBONARA

We actually prefer boxed pasta for this classic dish because it seems to retain more heat and so achieves the final cooking of the eggs more effectively. If prosciutto is unavailable, substitute smoked ham or Canadian bacon (cook the Canadian bacon for a few minutes with the onions).

—— SERVES 4-6 ——

3 extra-large eggs

½ cup freshly grated Parmesan, plus more for serving

⅓ pound bacon

Salt

2 tablespoons vegetable oil

1 pound spaghetti

1 medium red onion, roughly chopped

½ cup prosciutto—or smoked ham or Canadian bacon, julienned (optional)

3 tablespoons heavy cream

¼ cup chopped fresh parsley

Freshly ground pepper

1. In a small bowl, beat the eggs and stir in the Parmesan. Set aside.

2. In a large skillet, cook the bacon until all the fat is rendered but the bacon is not altogether crisp. Remove with a slotted spoon and drain on paper towels. When the bacon has cooled, crumble it into small pieces and set aside.

3. In a stockpot, bring 5 quarts of water to a boil and add 1 tablespoon of salt and the vegetable oil. Add the spaghetti, stir, and cook until al dente. Drain thoroughly.

4. While the pasta is cooking, remove all but 2 tablespoons of bacon fat from the skillet and cook the onion over medium-high heat until just barely softened. Add the prosciutto, if using, stir, and turn off the heat.

5. You must move very quickly through this step. As soon as the pasta is drained, transfer it to the skillet, add the egg and cheese mixture, and toss until the strands are coated. Add the cream, parsley, bacon, the onion and prosciutto mixture, ½ teaspoon of salt, and pepper to taste. Toss again and serve with a bowl of freshly grated Parmesan on the side.

RAVIOLI WITH DRIED MUSHROOMS AND CREAM

This and the sauce opposite are to be served with ravioli stuffed with spinach and cheese, either purchased from a specialty shop or, if you have the time, homemade (we use the recipe in Ada Boni's Italian Regional Cooking*). Both sauces are also good with any flat pasta. In most major cities, good fresh ravioli is available at pasta shops.*

—— SERVES 4-6 ——

1 ounce dried porcini
  mushrooms

1 cup hot water

2 tablespoons butter

1 cup heavy cream

¼ cup freshly grated
  Parmesan, plus more for
  serving

Freshly ground pepper

1¼ pounds ravioli

1. In a small bowl, soak the mushrooms in the hot water for 1 hour. Remove the mushrooms from the liquid and chop fine. Line a sieve with several layers of cheesecloth and strain the liquid through the sieve into a small skillet. Add the mushrooms and reduce the liquid over medium heat until there are only 2 tablespoons.

2. Add the butter and cream to the reduced liquid and bring the mixture to a boil over medium heat. Boil gently for a few minutes, until the sauce thickens. Remove from the heat and stir in the Parmesan. Add pepper to taste.

3. When the sauce is done, drop the ravioli into 5 quarts of boiling water to which you have added 1 tablespoon of salt and 2 tablespoons of vegetable oil. The ravioli will be cooked shortly after they rise to the surface of the water. Start checking after 1 minute—cooking time depends on the freshness of the ravioli. When done, drain carefully to avoid breakage, and toss—again, carefully—with the sauce. Serve in heated bowls with a bowl of freshly grated Parmesan on the side.

RAVIOLI WITH ANCHOVIES, GARLIC, AND CREAM

— SERVES 4–6 —

2 tablespoons butter

6 anchovy fillets, chopped

1 clove garlic, minced

1 cup heavy cream

¼ cup freshly grated
  Parmesan cheese, plus more
  for serving

Freshly ground pepper

1¼ pounds ravioli

1. In a small skillet, heat the butter over medium-low heat. Add the anchovies and garlic, and cook, mashing the anchovies with a wooden spoon for about 2 minutes.

2. Add the cream, raise the heat to medium, and boil gently for a few minutes until the sauce thickens. Remove from the heat and stir in the Parmesan. Add pepper to taste.

3. Following the directions on page 188, cook the ravioli and drain. In a large bowl, carefully toss the ravioli with the sauce and serve in heated bowls with freshly grated Parmesan on the side.

FETTUCCINE WITH FRESH AND DRIED MUSHROOMS, CHICKEN, AND CREAM

1 ounce dried porcini
  mushrooms

1 cup hot water

3 tablespoons butter

1 small onion, minced

¾ pound fresh mushrooms,
  chopped

1½ cups heavy cream

4 chicken thighs, poached,
  skinned, and shredded
  (about 1½ cups), or use
  leftover cooked chicken
  (see Double Consommé with
  Mushrooms, page 8)

1 tablespoon salt

2 tablespoons vegetable oil

1 pound fettuccine

¼ cup chopped fresh
  parsley

½ cup freshly grated
  Parmesan, plus more for
  serving

Freshly ground pepper

1. In a small bowl, soak the mushrooms in the hot water for
1 hour. Remove the mushrooms from the liquid and chop fine.
Line a sieve with several layers of cheesecloth and strain the liquid
through the sieve into a small saucepan. Add the soaked dried
mushrooms, bring to a boil, and reduce until only 1 tablespoon of
liquid remains, about 5 minutes. Set aside.

2. In a large skillet, melt the butter over medium heat, add the
onion, and cook for a few minutes. Add the fresh mushrooms
and sauté until their liquid has evaporated and the mushrooms
are lightly browned. Add the soaked dried mushrooms and their
reduced liquid.

3. Add the cream and chicken to the skillet and boil gently until
the cream thickens, about 5 minutes. Turn off the heat.

4. While you are reducing the cream, in a stockpot bring 5 quarts of water to a boil and add the salt and vegetable oil. Add the fettuccine, stir, and cook until al dente. Drain thoroughly.

5. In a bowl, toss the pasta with the sauce, add the parsley, Parmesan, and pepper to taste, and toss again. Serve in heated bowls with grated Parmesan on the side.

PENNE WITH BLACK OLIVE PURÉE AND RICOTTA

We first had this pasta at the Gamela restaurant in Rome. The black olive purée gives the sauce an unusual color, and its very rich taste makes it best served as a first course.

—— SERVES 8 ——

½ cup ricotta cheese

½ cup heavy cream

¾ cup purée of black Italian or Greek olives (Kalamata or Gaeta)

½ cup freshly grated Parmesan, plus more for serving

2 tablespoons butter, at room temperature

1 tablespoon salt

2 tablespoons vegetable oil

1 pound penne

¼ cup finely chopped fresh parsley

Freshly ground pepper

1. In a small saucepan, blend the ricotta and heavy cream over very low heat until smooth. Remove from the heat and stir in the olive purée and the Parmesan. Place the butter, cut into small pieces, in a large bowl.

2. In a stockpot, bring 5 quarts of water to a boil and add the salt and vegetable oil. Add the penne, stir, and cook until al dente. Drain thoroughly.

3. Place the pasta in the large bowl and toss with the butter. Add the cheese/olive purée and toss. Add the parsley and pepper to taste and toss again.

4. Serve in heated bowls with a bowl of freshly grated Parmesan on the side.

FUSILLI WITH ASPARAGUS, PARSLEY, AND CREAM

— SERVES 4–6 —

10 medium asparagus spears, trimmed to about 4 inches

6 tablespoons butter

¼ cup olive oil

1 cup finely chopped fresh parsley

3 cloves garlic, finely chopped

½ teaspoon red pepper flakes

1 cup heavy cream

¼ cup freshly grated Parmesan, plus more for serving

Salt and freshly ground pepper

2 tablespoons vegetable oil

1 pound fusilli

1. In a saucepan, bring 2 cups of water to a boil, add the asparagus, and cook until it is just tender at the base end. Drain the asparagus, run under cold water, and dry on paper towels. Cut into ¼-inch slices and set aside.

2. In a large skillet, melt the butter, add the oil, parsley, garlic, and red pepper flakes, and cook over medium heat for about 2 minutes, stirring.

3. Add the cream and continue to cook, stirring constantly, until it has reduced a little—about 5 minutes. Remove from the heat and stir in the Parmesan and salt and pepper to taste.

4. In the meantime, in a stockpot, bring 5 quarts of water to a boil and add 1 tablespoon of salt and the vegetable oil. Add the fusilli, stir, and cook until not quite al dente. Drain well, add to the saucepan, and continue to cook for 2 minutes, making sure the fusilli are well coated with the cream mixture. Add the asparagus and heat through. Serve in heated bowls with a bowl of freshly grated Parmesan on the side.

FETTUCCINE WITH PROSCIUTTO, ASPARAGUS, AND CREAM

This is best made with delicate, young asparagus, although it is still delicious with the larger stalks. We first had a version of this sauce at the Umbria restaurant in Todi, where they make it with tiny wild asparagus.

— SERVES 4–6 —

1 pound asparagus

Salt

2 tablespoons vegetable oil

1 pound fettuccine

3 tablespoons butter

3 tablespoons minced onion

2 cloves garlic, minced

1/3 cup shredded prosciutto

1 cup heavy cream

Pinch freshly grated nutmeg

Freshly ground pepper

1/2 cup freshly grated Parmesan, plus more for serving

1 egg yolk

1. Cut the tough ends off the asparagus. If they are not the very thin, early asparagus (with a diameter of no more than 1/4 inch), peel the stalks below the tip. Fill a 10-inch skillet with 5 cups of water and add 1 tablespoon of salt. Bring to a boil, add the asparagus, and cook until barely tender, 5 to 10 minutes, depending on the thickness of the asparagus. Drain.

2. Cut the tips off the asparagus and set aside. Cut the stalks in half lengthwise (in quarters, if thick) and cut the strips into 1-inch lengths. Set aside.

3. In a stockpot, bring 5 quarts of water to a boil and add 1 tablespoon of salt and the vegetable oil. Add the fettuccine, stir, and cook until al dente. (If you are using fresh pasta, proceed with the recipe while the water is heating. If you are using dried pasta, proceed after you have put the pasta in the water to cook.)

4. Meanwhile, in a skillet, melt the butter over medium-low heat, add the onion, and cook until soft. Add the garlic and prosciutto for the last minute of cooking.

5. Add the asparagus, turning it for a minute or so in the butter. Add the cream and the nutmeg, turn the heat up to medium-high, and cook, stirring occasionally, until the cream has thickened, about 5 minutes. Turn off the heat and add salt and pepper to taste.

6. In a small bowl, beat 1 tablespoon of the Parmesan into the egg yolk, then carefully fold the egg yolk mixture into the sauce.

7. Drain the pasta and place in a heated serving bowl. Toss with the asparagus sauce and the remaining Parmesan. Serve in heated bowls, with a bowl of freshly grated Parmesan on the side.

FUSILLI WITH ASPARAGUS, TOMATOES, AND EGGS

— SERVES 4 —

2 large eggs

⅓ cup freshly grated
  Parmesan, plus more for
  serving

Salt and freshly ground pepper

4 tablespoons butter

1 pound fresh asparagus,
  trimmed and cut into
  ½-inch slices

2 tablespoons olive oil

3 cloves garlic, mashed

1½ cups canned Italian
  tomatoes, drained, seeded,
  and chopped

3 tablespoons chopped fresh
  parsley

2 tablespoons vegetable oil

1 pound fusilli

1. In a small bowl, beat together the eggs, Parmesan, and salt and pepper to taste and set aside.

2. In a large skillet, melt 3 tablespoons of the butter over low heat, add the asparagus pieces, and cook covered, until just tender, about 10 minutes. Remove to a dish and reserve.

3. Add the oil and the remaining tablespoon of butter to the skillet and, when the butter is hot, sauté the garlic. When the garlic begins to turn brown, remove and discard it.

4. Add the tomatoes and parsley to the skillet and simmer over low heat, uncovered, for 10 minutes. Then add the asparagus and cook for another 5 minutes.

5. In a stockpot, bring 5 quarts of water to a boil and add 1 tablespoon of salt and the vegetable oil. Add the fusilli, stir, and cook until al dente. Drain thoroughly. Time the pasta so it will be ready when the asparagus and tomatoes have finished cooking.

6. In a serving bowl, toss the fusilli first with the egg/cheese mixture, then with the tomato/asparagus mixture. Serve with a bowl of freshly grated Parmesan on the side.

FETTUCCINE WITH PROSCIUTTO, MUSHROOMS, AND PEAS

½ pound bacon, cut into ¼-inch slices

3 tablespoons butter

1 tablespoon olive oil

¾ pound fresh mushrooms, sliced

2 cloves garlic, minced

½ cup heavy cream

1 cup young fresh peas or 1 cup frozen peas, defrosted

3 tablespoons chopped fresh parsley

¼ pound prosciutto, julienned (you may substitute smoked ham if absolutely necessary)

Salt and freshly ground pepper

2 tablespoons vegetable oil

1 pound fettuccine

½ cup grated Parmesan, plus more for serving

1. In a large skillet, fry the bacon until crisp and drain on paper towels.

2. Add the butter and oil to the skillet and when the butter is sizzling, add the mushrooms. Cook until their liquid is released, stirring occasionally to prevent scorching. Turn up the heat and cook until that liquid has evaporated, another 3 or 4 minutes. Add the garlic, cream, peas, 1 tablespoon of the chopped fresh parsley, the prosciutto, and salt and pepper to taste. Cook until the cream has thickened, about 5 minutes.

3. Meanwhile, in a stockpot, bring 5 quarts of water to a boil and add 1 tablespoon of salt and the vegetable oil. Add the fettuccine, stir, and cook until al dente. Drain thoroughly and place in a serving bowl. Toss with the Parmesan and then with the sauce (reheated if necessary). Try to time it so the sauce and the pasta are finished at the same time. Garnish with the remaining 2 tablespoons of chopped fresh parsley and serve immediately.

CONCHIGLIE WITH SPINACH, BASIL, AND RICOTTA

— SERVES 6-8 —

2 pounds fresh spinach, or two 10-ounce boxes frozen chopped spinach, thoroughly defrosted

6 tablespoons butter

6 scallions, white part only, minced

2 cloves garlic, minced

Salt and freshly ground pepper

1/4 teaspoon freshly grated nutmeg

2 tablespoons vegetable oil

1 pound conchiglie (small shells)

1 cup ricotta cheese

1/4 cup heavy cream

1/2 cup chopped fresh basil or parsley

1/2 cup freshly grated Parmesan, plus more for serving

1. If you are using fresh spinach, wash it carefully and place it in a large stainless steel pot with the water that clings to the leaves from washing. Cook over medium-low heat until the spinach is wilted, stirring occasionally. Drain in a colander, and when cool enough to handle, squeeze out the excess liquid. Chop fine. If you are using frozen spinach, squeeze the excess liquid out of the defrosted spinach and chop it again. Set aside.

2. In a stainless steel skillet, melt 4 tablespoons of the butter. Add the scallions and garlic and sauté over medium-low heat for 1 minute. Add the spinach and sprinkle with 1/2 teaspoon of salt, pepper to taste, and the nutmeg. Sauté over low heat for a few minutes, until the spinach is heated through. Set aside.

3. In a stockpot, bring 5 quarts of water to a boil and add 1 tablespoon of salt and the vegetable oil. Add the conchiglie, stir, and cook the pasta until al dente. Drain thoroughly.

4. While the pasta is cooking, blend the ricotta and cream in a small saucepan and heat over very low heat until smooth. In a large serving bowl, soften the remaining 2 tablespoons of butter with a wooden spoon. Add the pasta and toss it with the butter. Add the ricotta/cream mixture, spinach (reheat if necessary), basil, and Parmesan and combine well. Serve with a bowl of freshly grated Parmesan on the side.

PENNE WITH BROCCOLI, BACON, AND ANCHOVIES

5 cloves garlic, chopped

6 anchovy fillets, drained, rinsed, and chopped

1 tablespoon olive oil

1 teaspoon coarse sea salt

6 slices of bacon, cut into ¼-inch slices

1 head broccoli, cut into small florets

1 tablespoon salt

2 tablespoons vegetable oil

1 pound of penne rigate (ribbed penne)

½ cup freshly grated Parmesan, plus more for serving

1. In a small bowl, combine the garlic, anchovies, olive oil, and coarse salt and mash into a paste with a wooden spoon.

2. In a large heavy skillet, cook the bacon over medium heat until it begins to get crisp. Lower the heat and add the anchovy/garlic mixture. Stir for 4 or 5 minutes, until the anchovies have liquefied and the garlic has colored slightly.

3. Add the broccoli to the skillet and cook over high heat, stirring constantly to prevent burning, until the broccoli has softened and turned a dark green, but is still crunchy.

4. In a stockpot, bring 5 quarts of water to a boil and add the 1 tablespoon of salt and the vegetable oil. Add the penne, stir, and cook until al dente. Drain thoroughly and transfer to a large bowl. Add the Parmesan and the hot broccoli mixture to the pasta, toss, and serve with a bowl of freshly grated Parmesan on the side.

FUSILLI WITH ZUCCHINI, BACON, AND CREAM

4 slices of bacon, cut into
¼-inch slices

4 tablespoons butter

3 medium zucchini, cut in
half lengthwise and then
into ¼-inch slices

1 tablespoon salt

2 tablespoons vegetable oil

1 pound fusilli

½ cup freshly grated
Parmesan, plus more for
serving

¼ cup chopped fresh parsley

¼ cup heavy cream

1. In a large skillet, cook the bacon over medium-high heat until it is almost crisp. Add the butter and, when it is hot, add the zucchini and brown the pieces, stirring carefully.

2. In a stockpot, bring 5 quarts of water to a boil and add the salt and vegetable oil. Add the fusilli, stir, and cook until al dente. Drain thoroughly and transfer to a large bowl.

3. Add the Parmesan, parsley, and cream to the pasta and toss. Then add the zucchini mixture and toss gently, to keep the zucchini pieces intact. Serve with a bowl of freshly grated Parmesan on the side.

PENNE WITH CAULIFLOWER, GARLIC, AND OIL

As Marcella Hazan writes, "One of the basic mother sauces for pasta is aglio e olio, *garlic and oil. From it has been spawned a multitudinous brood of sauces wherein we find most varieties of vegetables." This particular descendant—a perfect blend of cauliflower, anchovies, garlic, and oil—is hers.*

— SERVES 4-6 —

1 head cauliflower, about 1¼ pounds

½ cup olive oil

2 large cloves garlic, minced

6 anchovy fillets, chopped

¼ teaspoon chopped hot red pepper, or red pepper flakes

Salt

1 pound penne

2 tablespoons chopped fresh parsley

Freshly grated Parmesan

1. Strip the cauliflower of all its leaves, except for a few of the very tender inner ones. Rinse it in cold water and cut it in half lengthwise.

2. In a saucepan, bring 4 to 5 quarts of water to a boil, then put in the cauliflower. Cook until tender, but firm—25 to 30 minutes. Test it with a fork to determine when it is done. Drain and set aside.

3. In a medium sauté pan, combine the oil, garlic, and chopped anchovies. Turn the heat to medium, and sauté until the garlic becomes a golden brown. Stir from time to time with a wooden spoon, mashing the anchovies with it.

4. Add the boiled cauliflower and break it up quickly with a fork, crumbling it into pieces no bigger than a peanut. Turn it thoroughly in the oil, mashing part of it to a pulp.

5. Add the hot pepper and 1 tablespoon salt. Raise the heat and cook for a few minutes more, stirring frequently. Then turn off the heat.

6. In a stockpot, bring 5 quarts of water to a boil, add a liberal amount of salt, and as soon as the water returns to a boil, put in the pasta. When cooked until al dente, drain it well and transfer it to a warmed serving bowl.

7. Very briefly reheat the cauliflower, and pour all the contents of the pan over the pasta. Toss thoroughly. Add the chopped parsley, toss again, and serve at once, with a bowl of freshly grated Parmesan on the side.

BUCATINI WITH ESCAROLE, ANCHOVIES, AND CREAM

— SERVES 4-6 —

Salt

1 head escarole, chopped

3 tablespoons olive oil

3 tablespoons butter

1 medium onion, finely chopped

8 anchovy fillets, chopped

3 cloves garlic, minced

2 tablespoons vegetable oil

1 pound bucatini

½ cup heavy cream

Freshly ground pepper

½ cup freshly grated Parmesan, plus more for serving

1. In a stockpot, bring 2 quarts of water to a boil and add 1 tablespoon of salt. Add the escarole and cook until tender, about 5 minutes. Drain in a colander and press the escarole against the sides of the colander with a wooden spoon to remove excess liquid. Set aside.

2. In a large skillet, heat the oil and butter. Add the onion and sauté over medium-low heat until tender. Add the anchovies and garlic and cook, mashing the anchovies with a wooden spoon until they form a paste.

3. In a stockpot, bring 5 quarts of water to a boil and add 1 tablespoon of salt and the vegetable oil. Add the bucatini, stir, and cook until al dente. Drain thoroughly.

4. While the bucatini is cooking, add the escarole to the onion/ anchovy mixture and cook over medium heat for a few minutes, tossing the escarole. Add the cream and a generous grinding of pepper and cook, stirring, for a few minutes, or until the cream is slightly thickened. Add salt to taste.

5. In a large bowl, toss the bucatini with the escarole mixture and the Parmesan. Serve with a bowl of freshly grated Parmesan on the side.

FUSILLI WITH CARROTS, PROSCIUTTO, AND CREAM

—— SERVES 4-6 ——

5 tablespoons butter

1 small onion, finely chopped

6 carrots, peeled and grated

⅓ cup shredded prosciutto

1 cup heavy cream

¼ cup chopped fresh parsley

Salt and freshly ground pepper

2 tablespoons vegetable oil

1 pound fusilli

½ cup freshly grated Parmesan, plus more for serving

1. In a small skillet, melt the butter. Add the onion and sauté over medium-low heat until barely tender. Add the carrots, stir to coat them with the butter, and cook, stirring occasionally, until the carrots are tender, about 10 minutes.

2. Add the prosciutto, stir to coat it with the butter, and cook for 30 seconds. Add the cream, raise the heat to medium, and cook, stirring, until the cream thickens, about 5 minutes. Turn off the heat, stir in the parsley, and add salt and pepper to taste.

3. In a stockpot, bring 5 quarts of water to a boil and add 1 tablespoon of salt and the vegetable oil. Add the fusilli, stir, and cook until al dente. Drain thoroughly.

4. In a large bowl, toss the pasta with the sauce (reheated if necessary) and the Parmesan. Serve in heated bowls with a bowl of freshly grated Parmesan on the side.

LINGUINE PRIMAVERA

*A variation on the pasta served at Dušan Bernić's Terrace
restaurant in New York City.*

Salt

1 head broccoli, cut in tiny florets

1 pound asparagus, trimmed and cut in ¼-inch diagonal slices

1 zucchini, thinly sliced

½ cup fresh peas

8 tablespoons softened butter

2 tablespoons minced fresh basil (or 2 teaspoons dried basil)

1 teaspoon minced fresh summer savory (or ⅓ teaspoon dried summer savory)

1 teaspoon minced fresh tarragon (or ½ teaspoon dried tarragon)

3 tablespoons olive oil

½ pound fresh mushrooms, sliced

2 cloves garlic, minced

½ medium onion, minced

½ teaspoon red pepper flakes

¼ cup Chicken Stock (page 5)

½ cup heavy cream

2 tablespoons vegetable oil

1 pound linguine

½ cup freshly grated Parmesan

1 tomato, chopped

3 tablespoons chopped fresh parsley

1. Bring a large pot of salted water to a fast boil. Drop in the broccoli, asparagus, zucchini, and peas, and cook for 30 seconds, drain, and refresh under cold water to prevent the vegetables from continuing to cook. Drain again and remove to a bowl.

2. In a large serving bowl, combine the softened butter, basil, summer savory, and tarragon and set aside.

3. In a large skillet, heat the olive oil; add the mushrooms and cook for 2 minutes. Transfer to the bowl with the vegetables. Add the garlic, onion, and red pepper flakes to the skillet and cook over medium heat for 2 to 3 minutes. Add the stock and cook for 3 minutes, to reduce it slightly. Add the cream and continue cooking until it thickens slightly. Remove from the heat until ready to add the sauce to the pasta.

4. In a stockpot, bring 5 quarts of water to a boil and add 1 tablespoon of salt and the vegetable oil. Add the linguine, stir, and cook until al dente.

5. While the pasta is cooking, add the vegetables to the cream mixture and heat them so they are ready when the linguine is done. Drain the linguine and place it in the bowl with the butter/ herb mixture. Toss quickly to melt the butter. Then add the sauce with the heated vegetables, the Parmesan, tomato, and parsley, toss, and serve.

FETTUCCELLE WITH SCALLOPS AND CREAM

— SERVES 4-6 —

1 egg

½ cup heavy cream

Salt

2 tablespoons vegetable oil

1 pound fettuccelle

4 tablespoons butter

4 cloves garlic, minced

¼ cup finely chopped fresh
  parsley

½ teaspoon red pepper flakes

2 pints sea scallops,
  quartered, or bay scallops

Freshly ground pepper

Garnish: chopped fresh
  parsley

1. In a small bowl, beat the egg into the cream and set aside.

2. In a stockpot, bring 5 quarts of water to a boil and add
1 tablespoon of salt and the vegetable oil. Add the fettuccelle, stir,
and cook until al dente.

3. Meanwhile, in a flameproof casserole large enough to hold
the pasta, melt the butter over medium-low heat. Add the garlic,
parsley, and red pepper flakes and cook, stirring constantly, for
about 2 minutes. Add the scallops and cook over medium heat
for 2 minutes. Add salt and pepper to taste and remove from the
heat.

4. Thoroughly drain the fettuccelle and add it to the casserole
along with the egg/cream mixture. Let the sauce heat
through and thicken slightly, gently stirring to combine all the
ingredients—but do not let the sauce come to a boil or the egg
will curdle. Add salt and pepper to taste and garnish with the
chopped fresh parsley.

COLD FUSILLI WITH SCALLOPS, OLIVES, AND ROASTED RED PEPPERS

—— SERVES 4–6 ——

1 cup freshly squeezed lime juice

2 cloves garlic, minced

Peel of ½ lemon

¾ pound sea scallops, quartered

Salt and freshly ground pepper

2 tablespoons vegetable oil

1 pound fusilli

¼ cup olive oil

2 roasted red peppers, cut into 1 x ½-inch pieces

2 tablespoons capers

½ pound black olives (Kalamata if possible), pitted and quartered

2 tablespoons chopped fresh basil (do not use dried basil; if necessary, substitute parsley)

1. In a mixing bowl, combine the lime juice, garlic, lemon peel, and scallops. Cover and refrigerate for at least 5 hours.

2. When you are ready to prepare the fusilli, bring 5 quarts of water to a boil in a stockpot and add 1 tablespoon of salt and the vegetable oil. Add the fusilli, stir, and cook until al dente. Be sure not to overcook the fusilli; it is important that it remain firm. Drain thoroughly and place in a bowl. Toss with the olive oil and allow to come to room temperature.

3. In a large serving bowl, combine the red peppers, capers, olives, and salt and pepper to taste and toss gently. Remove the scallops from their liquid and add them to the serving bowl with the fusilli and basil. Toss again and serve immediately.

COLD TAGLIATELLE WITH POACHED SALMON IN CREAMY VINAIGRETTE

It is imperative that you use the thinnest pasta available for this dish.

—— SERVES 4-6 ——

COURT BOUILLON

4 cups dry white wine

1 onion, quartered

5 sprigs parsley

1 celery stalk, chopped

1 carrot, peeled and chopped

2 cloves garlic, smashed

5 peppercorns

2 pounds fresh salmon steaks

2 tablespoons white wine vinegar

2 tablespoons lemon juice

1 cup olive oil

2 tablespoons dry white wine

2 teaspoons Dijon mustard

Salt and freshly ground pepper

2 egg yolks

½ cup heavy cream

¼ cup finely chopped fresh parsley

¼ cup finely chopped fresh basil or tarragon (dry herbs won't work in this recipe)

2 tablespoons vegetable oil

1 pound tagliatelle (or capelli d'angelo)

2 fresh hot red peppers, finely chopped (or 1 sweet red pepper, skinned, seeded, and chopped)

Garnish: chopped fresh parsley

1. In a large skillet, combine the ingredients for the court bouillon and 4 cups of water. Bring to a boil and simmer, partially covered, for 30 minutes.

2. Add the salmon steaks to the skillet. There should be enough liquid to completely cover the salmon; if there is not enough, add water. Simmer, partially covered, until the fish flakes, about 7 minutes, and remove from the heat.

3. When the fish is cool enough to handle, remove to a plate, strain the liquid into a bowl, and reserve it. Now remove the skin and bones from the salmon, breaking up the fish into small pieces, and add the fish to the strained liquid. Reserve until you are ready to serve the dish.

4. In a small bowl, combine the vinegar, lemon juice, ¾ cup of the olive oil, white wine, mustard, and salt and pepper to taste. Set the vinaigrette aside.

5. In a food processor, blend the egg yolks and cream for 10 seconds and then, with the motor still running, add the vinaigrette in a very thin but steady stream. (This can also be done in a bowl using a whisk.) Remove to a bowl, stir in the parsley and basil or tarragon, and reserve.

6. When you are ready to serve the pasta, drain the salmon, putting the bouillon in the pot in which you are going to cook the pasta. Add an additional 3 quarts of cold water and bring to a boil, adding 1 tablespoon of salt and the vegetable oil. Add the tagliatelle, stir, and cook until al dente. Drain thoroughly and remove to a large serving bowl. Toss with the remaining ¼ cup of olive oil.

7. Add the salmon, red pepper, and creamy vinaigrette and toss until the pasta is well coated and the salmon is evenly distributed. Serve garnished with the chopped fresh parsley.

LINGUINE WITH WHITE CLAM SAUCE

20 cherrystone clams

4 tablespoons butter

8 shallots, finely chopped

6 cloves garlic, minced

2 tablespoons flour

½ cup dry white vermouth

½ cup heavy cream

1 teaspoon chopped fresh thyme (or ¼ teaspoon dried thyme)

¼ cup chopped fresh parsley

2 tablespoons chopped fresh basil (or 2 teaspoons dried basil)

Salt and freshly ground pepper

⅓ cup freshly grated Parmesan

2 tablespoons vegetable oil

1 pound linguine

Garnish: chopped fresh parsley

1. Wash the clams thoroughly. In a large flameproof casserole, bring 2 cups of water to a boil. Add the clams, cover, and steam the clams until they have opened, about 5 minutes. Remove from the heat, uncover, and allow to cool. Over a mixing bowl, open the shells, reserving their liquid, remove the clams, chop them, and reserve in a bowl. Strain the cooking liquid through a fine sieve lined with a double layer of cheesecloth into a small saucepan. Reduce the liquid over high heat to ½ cup and set aside.

2. In a large skillet, melt the butter over medium-low heat. Add the shallots and garlic and cook until soft. Add the flour and cook, without allowing the flour to brown, for 5 minutes. Add the reduced clam liquid, vermouth, and cream and cook over medium heat until the sauce thickens, stirring constantly. Remove from the heat.

3. Add the clams, thyme, parsley, basil, 1 teaspoon of salt, pepper to taste, and Parmesan and mix thoroughly over low heat for 3 minutes.

4. In a stockpot, bring 5 quarts of water to a boil and add 1 tablespoon of salt and the vegetable oil. Add the linguine, stir, and cook until al dente. Drain thoroughly, transfer to a bowl, and toss with the sauce (reheated if necessary). Serve garnished with the chopped fresh parsley.

LINGUINE WITH MUSSELS, TOMATOES, AND CREAM

This is an elegant first course. The tomato makes the sauce just slightly rosy, and the reduced court bouillon infuses the sauce with the bouquet of mussels and white wine. We have found that the often-suggested method of soaking mussels in cold water with cornmeal to encourage disgorging of sand is useless. If any sand remains in the mussel flesh after steaming, simply rinse them individually in a little of the cooking liquid.

—— SERVES 4-6 ——

3 pounds mussels

1 large onion, chopped

1 celery stalk, chopped

3 cloves garlic

2 sprigs parsley

½ teaspoon dried thyme

Freshly ground pepper

1½ cups dry white wine

2 tablespoons butter

1 small onion, finely chopped

2 tomatoes, peeled, seeded, and finely chopped

1 cup heavy cream

1 tablespoon salt

2 tablespoons vegetable oil

1 pound linguine

½ cup finely chopped fresh basil or parsley

1. Rinse the mussels under cold running water, rubbing the shells against each other to remove any encrustation. Remove the beards with a knife. Rinse the mussels well again under cold water and discard any that seem unusually heavy.

2. In a large stockpot, place the large onion, celery, 2 of the garlic cloves, bruised, the parsley sprigs, thyme, pepper to taste, and wine. Bring to a boil, lower the heat, and simmer, covered, for 15 minutes.

3. Raise the heat to medium-high and when the wine is boiling add all the mussels. Cover and cook until the mussels have opened, about 5 minutes, shaking the pot a couple of times.

4. Remove the mussels from the pot with a pair of tongs and place them in a large bowl. Then take the mussels out of their shells, place them in a bowl, and set aside. Discard any mussels that have not opened.

5. Strain the cooking liquid into a bowl, pouring it through a sieve lined with several layers of cheesecloth. Pour 3 tablespoons of the strained liquid over the reserved mussels and cover the bowl with plastic wrap. Pour the rest of the liquid into a small stainless steel saucepan and reduce the liquid over high heat until only ¼ cup remains.

6. In a small skillet, heat the butter over medium-low heat. Add the finely chopped onion and cook until tender but not browned. Mince the remaining garlic clove, and add it to the skillet along with the chopped tomatoes and cook, stirring, for 1 minute. Add the reduced cooking liquid and the cream, raise the heat to medium, and boil gently until the sauce has thickened slightly, about 5 minutes. Turn off the heat. Lift the mussels out of the bowl, leaving the liquid behind, and place them in the cream sauce.

7. In a stockpot, bring 5 quarts of water to a boil and add the salt and vegetable oil. Add the linguine, stir, and cook until al dente. Drain thoroughly.

8. While the pasta is cooking, heat the sauce and mussels very gently.

9. In a large bowl, toss the pasta with the sauce and the chopped fresh basil or parsley. Serve in heated bowls.

SPAGHETTI WITH MUSSELS, TOMATOES, AND BACON

— SERVES 4–6 —

3 pounds mussels

2 cups dry white wine

8 slices lean bacon, cut into ½-inch slices

1 medium onion, finely chopped

3 cloves garlic, minced

3 cups canned Italian tomatoes, drained, seeded, and chopped

1 teaspoon chopped fresh thyme (or ⅓ teaspoon dried thyme)

1 teaspoon red pepper flakes

Salt

2 tablespoons vegetable oil

1 pound spaghetti

¼ cup finely chopped fresh parsley

1. Rinse the mussels under cold running water, rubbing the shells against each other to remove any encrustation. Remove the beards with a sharp knife. Rinse the mussels well again under cold water and remove any that seem unusually heavy. In a large stockpot, bring 1 cup of water and 1 cup of the wine to a boil. Add the mussels, cover, and steam until the mussels have opened, about 5 minutes. Let cool and then transfer the mussels to a bowl with a slotted spoon, discarding those that did not open. Remove the meat from the shells, rinsing it in the cooking liquid to remove any sand, chop, and set aside. Return the liquid that collected in the bowl to the cooking liquid in the stockpot and strain all the liquid through a sieve lined with a double layer of cheesecloth. In a small saucepan, reduce the strained liquid to about ¼ cup and reserve.

2. In a large skillet, sauté the bacon until it is just crisp. Remove and drain on paper towels. Pour off about half of the fat and in the fat that remains, cook the onion and garlic until soft. Add the remaining cup of wine and cook over high heat until there is about ¼ cup of liquid remaining in the skillet.

3. Add the reserved mussel liquid, the tomatoes, thyme, and red pepper flakes and cook over medium heat for 20 minutes, stirring, until the mixture thickens slightly. Add the mussels, bacon, and salt to taste and continue cooking until the mussels have heated through.

4. In a stockpot, bring 5 quarts of water to a boil and add 1 tablespoon of salt and the vegetable oil. Add the spaghetti, stir, and cook until al dente. Drain thoroughly and toss in a large bowl with the mussels and tomato sauce and the chopped fresh parsley.

SPAGHETTI WITH TUNA FISH, ANCHOVIES, AND CAPERS

This pasta is both spicy and light, a pleasant change from sauces made with heavy cream and Parmesan. In the summer, you can eliminate the dried basil and substitute fresh basil for the parsley, and you can use peeled, seeded, and chopped fresh tomatoes instead of canned ones.

—— SERVES 4-6 ——

4 tablespoons olive oil

1 small onion, chopped fine

2 cloves garlic, minced

2 cups canned Italian tomatoes, drained, seeded, and chopped

½ teaspoon dried basil

2 tablespoons capers

Salt and freshly ground pepper

10 anchovy fillets, finely chopped

2 tablespoons butter, softened

One 6½-ounce can tuna fish

2 tablespoons vegetable oil

1 pound spaghetti

¼ cup chopped fresh parsley

1. In a saucepan, heat 3 tablespoons of the oil over medium-low heat. Add the onion and sauté until soft. Add the garlic for the last minute of cooking. Add the tomatoes and simmer, covered, for 15 minutes. Add the basil, capers, ½ teaspoon of salt, and pepper to taste and simmer for another 15 minutes.

2. While the tomatoes are cooking, mash the anchovies and butter together in a small bowl with a wooden spoon. Set aside. If the tuna is packed in olive oil, drain a tablespoon of the oil into a small skillet (discard the rest) and sauté the tuna over medium heat for 2 or 3 minutes, breaking it into small pieces. If the tuna is not packed in olive oil, drain it completely and sauté in the remaining tablespoon of olive oil. Set aside.

3. In a stockpot, bring 5 quarts of water to a boil and add 1 tablespoon of salt and the vegetable oil. Add the spaghetti, stir, and cook until al dente. Drain thoroughly.

4. In a bowl, toss the spaghetti with the tomato sauce, the anchovy butter, the tuna fish, and the chopped fresh parsley. Serve in heated bowls.

PENNE WITH SAUSAGE, MUSHROOMS, AND CREAM

½ ounce dried porcini mushrooms

1 cup hot water

6 hot Italian sausages

2 tablespoons olive oil

1 medium onion, chopped

2 cloves garlic, minced

½ pound fresh mushrooms, sliced

½ cup chopped fresh parsley

1 cup heavy cream

1 tablespoon salt

2 tablespoons vegetable oil

1 pound penne rigate (ribbed penne)

⅓ cup freshly grated Parmesan

Garnish: chopped fresh parsley

1. In a small bowl, cover the dried mushrooms with the hot water and let soak for 1 hour. Remove the mushrooms from the liquid, chop, and set aside. Strain the liquid through a sieve lined with several layers of cheesecloth and reserve.

2. Prick the skins of the sausages and in a heavy skillet cook them over medium-low heat in the olive oil until they are done, about 30 minutes. Remove to a plate. In the fat in the skillet, cook the onion for 10 minutes, without letting it brown, scraping up the sausage still clinging to the skillet. Add the garlic for the last minute of cooking.

3. Add the fresh mushrooms, raise the heat to medium, and cook for another 3 minutes.

4. Add the reserved soaked dried mushrooms and their liquid. Over high heat, stirring constantly, reduce the liquid to about 3 tablespoons.

5. Remove the sausage meat from the skins and crumble the cooked meat into the saucepan, along with the chopped parsley. Add the cream and cook, stirring frequently until the sauce thickens, about 5 minutes.

6. In a stockpot, bring 5 quarts of water to a boil and add the salt and vegetable oil. Add the penne, stir, and cook until al dente. Drain and transfer to a serving bowl. Toss with the Parmesan and then the sauce (reheated if necessary). Garnish with chopped fresh parsley.

PAPPARDELLE WITH CHICKEN LIVERS AND MUSHROOMS

— SERVES 4–6 —

1 pound chicken livers

2 tablespoons butter

2 tablespoons olive oil

5 scallions, white part only, minced

2 shallots, minced

2 cloves garlic, minced

½ pound fresh mushrooms, thinly sliced

½ cup dry vermouth

1 cup heavy cream

2 tomatoes, skinned, seeded, and chopped

½ teaspoon sugar

1 tablespoon chopped fresh basil (or 1 teaspoon dried basil)

½ teaspoon dried sage

Salt and freshly ground pepper

2 tablespoons vegetable oil

1 pound pappardelle (if you are not making your own pasta, substitute boxed fettuccine)

Garnish: chopped fresh parsley

1. Wash the chicken livers, removing the green spots and fat, and cut the livers into small pieces. Drain on a paper towel.

2. In a large skillet, heat the butter with the olive oil over medium heat. Add the scallions, shallots, and garlic and sauté for 3 minutes, being careful not to brown them. Add the livers and continue cooking until they have lost their raw color. With a slotted spoon, remove the mixture to a bowl.

3. In the same skillet, sauté the mushrooms over medium heat for 3 minutes, adding a little olive oil if the pan is too dry. Add the vermouth and reduce it to ¼ cup. Stir in the cream, tomatoes, sugar, basil, sage, and salt and pepper to taste and continue cooking until the liquid is reduced to ¾ cup.

4. Add the liver mixture and continue cooking, stirring, at a low simmer for 5 minutes.

5. Meanwhile, in a stockpot, bring 5 quarts of water to a boil and add 1 tablespoon of salt and the vegetable oil. Add the pappardelle, stir, and cook until al dente. Drain, place in a large serving bowl, and toss with the sauce (reheated if necessary). Garnish with the chopped fresh parsley and serve.

SPAGHETTI ALLA BOLOGNESE WITH MUSHROOMS

You must allow 5 hours to make this sauce, but it is well worth the time (most of which requires very little attention on your part). Since it freezes well, we often double the recipe and keep half on hand in the freezer, adding the heavy cream just before serving.

—— SERVES 4-6 ——

1 ounce dried porcini mushrooms

1 cup hot water

3 tablespoons butter

3 tablespoons olive oil

1 large onion, finely chopped

1 celery stalk, finely chopped

1 carrot, peeled and finely chopped

½ pound beef chuck, finely ground

½ pound pork shoulder, finely ground

2 cloves garlic, minced

1 cup dry white wine

1 cup Beef Stock (page 6)

2 cups canned Italian tomatoes, drained, seeded, and finely chopped

1 bay leaf

Salt and freshly ground pepper

¼ teaspoon freshly grated nutmeg

¼ cup heavy cream

2 tablespoons vegetable oil

1 pound spaghetti

½ cup freshly grated Parmesan, plus more for serving

1. In a small bowl, cover the dried mushrooms with the hot water and let soak for 1 hour. Lift the mushrooms out of the liquid, chop, and set aside. Strain the liquid through a sieve lined with several layers of cheesecloth. Set aside.

2. In a large saucepan, heat the butter and olive oil over medium-low heat. Add the onion, celery, and carrot and sauté until they begin to soften, about 5 minutes.

3. Raise the heat to medium and add the beef, pork, and garlic. Sauté, breaking up the meat with a wooden fork, until the meat is no longer red. Add the wine, raise the heat to high, and cook until the wine has almost completely evaporated.

4. Add the liquid from the soaked dried mushrooms, mushrooms, stock, tomatoes, and bay leaf. Simmer very gently, uncovered, for 4 hours, stirring only occasionally. If the sauce seems to be getting too thick after a few hours (this will depend on how gentle your simmer is), add a little more stock (if it is homemade) or water. Add salt and pepper to taste, the nutmeg, and cream and simmer for a few more minutes. Remove from the heat and remove the bay leaf.

5. In a stockpot, bring 5 quarts of water to a boil and add 1 tablespoon of salt and the vegetable oil. Add the spaghetti, stir, and cook until al dente. Drain thoroughly.

6. In a bowl, toss the pasta with the sauce (reheated if necessary) and the Parmesan. Serve with a bowl of freshly grated Parmesan on the side.

BAKED PENNE WITH EGGPLANT, TWO CHEESES, AND SALAMI

One summer evening at La Rosetta, in Perugia, a friend who is very knowledgeable about Italian food ordered this pasta, identified on the menu as macaroni Siciliana. We followed her lead and experienced one of our most satisfying meals in Italy—the pasta crusty along the edges from baking, moist and savory with the heady combination of eggplant and salami within. We serve it as either a first course or a main course. It is impossible to specify how much olive oil you will need to sauté the eggplant, but have plenty on hand.

—— SERVES 8 ——

3 large eggplants, unpeeled and cut into ¼-inch slices

Salt

Olive oil

4 tablespoons butter

1 small onion, finely chopped

3 cloves garlic, minced

4 cups canned Italian tomatoes, drained, seeded, and chopped

1 teaspoon dried basil

Freshly ground pepper

2 tablespoons vegetable oil

1 pound penne rigate (ribbed penne)

2 ounces Genoa salami, sliced and chopped

1¼ cups freshly grated Parmesan, plus more for serving

½ pound mozzarella cheese

⅓ cup bread crumbs

1. Sprinkle the eggplant slices liberally with salt, place in a colander, weight with a heavy plate, and let drain for 1 hour.

2. Rinse the eggplant quickly in water. Dry on paper towels, pressing down to extract the juices.

3. In a large skillet, heat 5 tablespoons of olive oil over medium-high heat. Add the eggplant slices in batches and sauté until they are brown on both sides. You will have to add more oil between batches. As they are done, remove the slices with a slotted spatula to drain on paper towels.

4. In a saucepan, melt 2 tablespoons of the butter. Add the onion and cook over medium-low heat until soft. Add the garlic for the last minute of cooking. Add the tomatoes and simmer very gently, partially covered, for 1 hour, stirring occasionally. Add the basil and simmer for another 10 minutes. Add pepper to taste.

5. Preheat the oven to 375°F.

6. In a stockpot, bring 5 quarts of water to a boil and add 1 tablespoon of salt and the vegetable oil. Add the penne, stir, and cook until not quite al dente, a bit on the chewy side (8 to 10 minutes for boxed pasta). Drain thoroughly, transfer to a large bowl, and toss with the tomato sauce, salami, and ¾ cup of the Parmesan.

7. Slice half the mozzarella as thin as possible. Set aside. Cut the rest of the mozzarella into small cubes and add to the penne.

8. Oil a rectangular enameled or porcelain baking dish, 14 x 9 x 2 inches. Scatter the bread crumbs over the bottom. Layer the eggplant, overlapping the slices, in the bottom. Chop the remaining eggplant and add it to the penne. Lay the slices of mozzarella over the layer of eggplant. Spoon the penne mixture over the mozzarella. Sprinkle the remaining ½ cup of Parmesan over the penne and dot with the remaining 2 tablespoons of butter.

9. Cover the baking dish with foil and bake for 20 minutes. Remove the foil and bake for another 20 minutes, or until the top is lightly browned.

BAKED LINGUINE WITH SALT COD, GARLIC, AND CREAM

This pasta is based on the classic brandade de morue, *a dish that inspires a deep and hidden passion in many people. Its humble ingredients are transformed in the finished purée to create a taste and texture that are indescribable.*

—— SERVES 6-8 ——

1 pound salt cod fillets

Juice of ½ lemon

1 small onion, sliced

1 bay leaf

4 cloves garlic, minced

¼ cup olive oil

1½ cups heavy cream

¼ cup finely chopped fresh parsley

Salt and freshly ground pepper

2 tablespoons vegetable oil

½ pound linguine

3 tablespoons butter

2 tablespoons freshly grated Parmesan, plus more for serving

1. Soak the salt cod overnight in cold water in the refrigerator. Change the water several times.

2. In a saucepan, combine 5 cups of cold water with the lemon juice, onion, and bay leaf. Bring to a boil, lower the heat, and simmer for 15 minutes. Add 2 cups of cold water and the salt cod. Just before the water comes to a simmer, remove from the heat. Cover and let the cod steep for 15 minutes. Remove with a slotted spoon, pick over the cod for bits of skin and bone, and break the cod into small pieces with your fingers.

3. Preheat the oven to 400°F.

4. In a food processor, pulse the cod and the garlic 2 or 3 times. With the motor running, gradually pour in the olive oil and cream.

5. Transfer the cod purée to a large bowl and stir in the chopped parsley. Add salt and pepper to taste.

6. In a stockpot, bring 5 quarts of water to a boil and add 1 tablespoon of salt and the vegetable oil. Add the linguine, stir, and cook until it is a little firmer than al dente (it will cook some more). Drain thoroughly.

7. Fold the linguine into the cod purée.

8. Use 1 tablespoon of the butter to grease a shallow oval baking dish with sides about 3 inches high. Spread the pasta and cod mixture in the dish, dot the top with the remaining 2 tablespoons of butter, and sprinkle the grated Parmesan over the mixture.

9. Bake until the top is golden and the casserole is bubbling around the edges, about 15 minutes.

LASAGNE WITH SAUSAGE, SPINACH, RICOTTA, AND TOMATO

10 tablespoons olive oil

1 medium onion, finely chopped

1 carrot, finely chopped

2 cloves garlic, minced

4 cups canned Italian tomatoes, drained, seeded, and chopped

1 teaspoon sugar

1 teaspoon dried basil

1½ pounds sweet Italian sausage

½ cup dry white wine

Salt and freshly ground pepper

1 egg

1 pound ricotta cheese

One 10-ounce package frozen chopped spinach, thoroughly defrosted

¼ teaspoon freshly grated nutmeg

1½ cups freshly grated Parmesan

2 tablespoons vegetable oil

1 pound lasagne

1. In a saucepan, heat 3 tablespoons of the olive oil. Add the onion and carrot and sauté over medium-low heat until soft, about 10 minutes. Add the garlic for the last minute of cooking. Add the tomatoes and sugar, bring to a boil, and simmer very gently, partially covered, for 1 hour. Add the basil and simmer for another 10 minutes. Set the sauce aside.

2. Remove the sausage meat from the casing. In a large skillet, heat 2 tablespoons of olive oil. Add the sausage meat and sauté over medium heat, breaking up the lumps with a fork, until the fat is rendered and the meat is lightly browned, about 30 minutes. Drain off most of the fat. Add the wine to the skillet, raise the heat to high, and cook until it has evaporated.

3. Preheat the oven to 350°F.

4. Set aside ½ cup of the tomato sauce. Add the rest to the skillet and simmer for 1 or 2 minutes. Add salt and pepper to taste.

5. In a small bowl, beat the egg lightly, then blend it with the ricotta. Squeeze out all the excess liquid from the defrosted spinach, chop it fine, and add it to the ricotta. Stir in the nutmeg and 1 cup of the Parmesan.

6. In a stockpot, bring 7 quarts of water to a boil and add 1 tablespoon of salt and the vegetable oil. Add the lasagne, stir, and cook until not quite al dente, a bit on the chewy side (8 to 10 minutes for boxed pasta). Holding a slotted spoon at the edge of the pot, pour out most of the hot water and fill the pot with cold water. Carefully remove the lasagne strips and lay them on paper towels.

7. With 1 tablespoon of olive oil, coat a rectangular baking dish that measures approximately 14 x 9 x 2 inches. Place a layer of lasagne strips on the bottom of the dish, overlapping slightly, not more than ⅛ inch. Cut the strips if they extend beyond the length of the dish; do not bring them up around the edges. Over the layer of lasagne, spread one third of the ricotta mixture. Over the ricotta mixture, spread one third of the sausage/tomato sauce. Make 2 more layers of lasagne, ricotta mixture, and sausage/tomato sauce, and top with a layer of lasagne. Spread over it the reserved ½ cup of tomato sauce and sprinkle with the remaining ½ cup of Parmesan. Drizzle the remaining 4 tablespoons of olive oil over the top. Bake until the lasagne is bubbling and the top is nicely browned, about 40 minutes. Let the lasagne stand for 10 minutes before serving.

LASAGNE WITH CHICKEN, ARTICHOKES, AND MUSHROOMS

—— SERVES 6-8 ——

1 medium onion, chopped

1 celery stalk, chopped

1 carrot, peeled and chopped

3 sprigs parsley

2 large chicken breasts, split

Salt

1 ounce dried porcini
mushrooms

1 cup hot water

One 9-ounce package frozen
artichoke hearts, thoroughly
defrosted

9 tablespoons butter

1 teaspoon lemon juice

1 pound fresh mushrooms,
chopped

1/4 cup minced shallots

2 cloves garlic, minced

Freshly ground pepper

1 egg

1 1/2 cups heavy cream

1 1/2 cups ricotta cheese

1/4 teaspoon freshly grated
nutmeg

1/2 cup chopped fresh parsley

2 tablespoons vegetable oil

1 pound spinach lasagne

1/2 cup shredded prosciutto or
ham

1/3 pound Asiago or Gruyère
cheese, cut into 1/4-inch dice

1 1/2 cups freshly grated
Parmesan

1. In a large saucepan, cover the onion, celery, carrot, and parsley sprigs with 8 cups of water and bring to a boil, then lower the heat and simmer for 15 minutes. Add the chicken and 1/2 teaspoon of salt. Simmer slowly until the chicken is cooked, about 30 minutes. Let the chicken cool in the liquid. Remove the meat from the bones, tear it into bite-size pieces, and set aside. If you like, you may put the skin and bones back in the liquid, simmer for 1 hour, drain the stock, and reserve it for another purpose.

2. In a small bowl, soak the dried mushrooms in the hot water for 1 hour. Remove the mushrooms from the liquid and chop. Strain the liquid through a sieve lined with several layers of cheesecloth into a small saucepan. Add the mushrooms to the liquid, bring to a boil, and cook until the liquid has almost entirely evaporated. Set aside.

3. Preheat the oven to 350°F.

4. Cut the artichokes into quarters lengthwise. Melt 2 tablespoons of the butter in a small skillet, add the artichokes, and sauté over medium-low heat until tender, about 5 minutes. Turn off the heat, toss the artichokes with the lemon juice, and set aside.

5. In a large skillet, melt 5 tablespoons of the butter. Over medium-high heat, sauté the fresh mushrooms until they have given up their liquid and are lightly browned. Add the shallots, garlic, and soaked dried mushrooms for the last minute of cooking. Add salt and pepper to taste and set aside.

6. In a bowl, beat the egg lightly and add ½ cup of the cream. Blend the ricotta into the egg/cream mixture and add the nutmeg and chopped parsley. Set aside.

7. In a stockpot, bring 7 quarts of water to a boil and add 1 tablespoon of salt and the vegetable oil. Add the lasagne, stir, and cook until not quite al dente, a bit on the chewy side (8 to 10 minutes for boxed pasta). Holding a slotted spoon at the edge of the pot, pour out most of the hot water and fill the pot with cold water. Carefully remove the lasagne strips and lay them on paper towels.

8. With 1 tablespoon of the butter, coat a rectangular baking dish that measures approximately 14 x 9 x 2 inches. Place a layer of lasagne strips on the bottom of the dish, overlapping slightly, not more than ⅛ inch. Cut the strips if they extend beyond the length of the dish; do not bring them up around the edges. On the layer of lasagne, lay one third of the chicken, one third of the

(continued)

artichokes, one third of the mushrooms, one third of the ricotta mixture, one third of the prosciutto, and one third of the Asiago or Gruyère. Sprinkle with ⅓ cup of the Parmesan and salt and pepper. Make 2 more layers and top with a layer of lasagne. Pour the remaining 1 cup of cream over the top. Sprinkle the remaining ½ cup of the Parmesan over the top and dot with the remaining 1 tablespoon butter.

9. Bake until the lasagne is bubbling and lightly browned, about 40 minutes. Let the lasagne stand for 10 minutes before serving.

FUSILLI WITH RED CAVIAR, FENNEL, AND CREAM

We suggest you use salmon roe (believing that the precious sturgeon eggs should be eaten pure); red lumpfish roe may be substituted, but the taste is definitely inferior. The fennel leaves impart a marvelous flavor, but fresh dill, which is easier to come by, is almost as good.

— SERVES 6 —

¼ cup freshly grated Parmesan

1 egg yolk

1 tablespoon salt

2 tablespoons vegetable oil

1 pound fusilli

2 tablespoons butter

1 cup heavy cream

¼ cup chopped fennel leaves or fresh dill

⅓ cup salmon roe

Freshly ground pepper

Freshly grated Parmesan

1. In a small bowl, beat 1 tablespoon of the Parmesan into the egg yolk and set aside.

2. In a stockpot, bring 5 quarts of water to a boil and add the salt and vegetable oil. Add the fusilli, stir, and cook until al dente. Drain thoroughly and place in a large bowl.

3. Meanwhile, in a small skillet, melt the butter over medium heat, add the cream, and cook, stirring, until slightly thickened, about 5 minutes. Turn off the heat and let the sauce sit for 2 or 3 minutes. Then stir in the egg yolk mixture, the remaining 3 tablespoons of Parmesan, the fennel or dill, and salmon roe.

4. Add the sauce to the bowl and toss with the pasta. Add pepper to taste.

5. Serve in heated bowls with a bowl of freshly grated Parmesan on the side.

BAKED FUSILLI WITH CHEESE, PARSLEY, AND SCALLIONS

A variation on the classic American macaroni and cheese, this makes a fine Sunday night supper when followed by a green salad. We prefer the texture of the fusilli, and it catches the bits of parsley, scallion, and cheese.

— SERVES 8 —

Salt

2 tablespoons vegetable oil

1 pound fusilli

3 eggs

1½ cups milk

⅓ cup chopped fresh parsley

⅓ cup minced scallions, with 1 inch of the green

Pinch cayenne pepper

1½ pounds white cheddar cheese, grated

1 tablespoon butter

¼ cup freshly grated Parmesan

¼ cup bread crumbs

1. Preheat the oven to 350°F.

2. In a stockpot, bring 5 quarts of water to a boil and add 1 tablespoon of salt and the vegetable oil. Add the fusilli, stir, and cook until not quite al dente. Drain thoroughly.

3. In a large bowl, beat the eggs lightly and then stir in the milk. Add the parsley, scallions, cayenne, and 1 teaspoon of salt. Add the fusilli and toss. Fold in the cheddar.

4. With ½ tablespoon of the butter, coat a shallow rectangular baking dish, about 14 x 9 x 2 inches. Spoon the fusilli mixture into the baking dish. Sprinkle the Parmesan and the bread crumbs over the top and dot with the remaining butter.

5. Bake until the top is browned and the fusilli is bubbling, about 30 minutes.

CHICKEN WITH FUSILLI, TOMATOES, AND ROSEMARY

In this dish, the pasta is the first course and the chicken is served afterward as a main course, accompanied by a green vegetable.

—— SERVES 4 ——

One 4-pound chicken

¼ lemon

Salt and freshly ground
  pepper

½ onion

1 bay leaf

3 tablespoons olive oil

3 tablespoons butter

1 large leek, white part only,
  cleaned and sliced

1 teaspoon dried rosemary

2 cloves garlic, minced

1 cup dry white wine

1 cup canned Italian
  tomatoes, drained, seeded,
  and chopped

1 cup Chicken Stock (page 5)

2 tablespoons vegetable oil

2 tablespoons fresh parsley

¾ pound fusilli

Freshly grated Parmesan

1. Rinse the chicken quickly under cold water. Dry thoroughly. Rub the cavity with the cut lemon, then sprinkle with salt and pepper to taste. Put the lemon, onion, and bay leaf in the cavity and truss the chicken.

2. In a flameproof casserole large enough to hold the chicken, heat the oil and 2 tablespoons of the butter and brown the chicken over medium heat on all sides, turning it carefully to avoid breaking the skin. This will take around 30 minutes. After 15 minutes, add the leek and rosemary and continue browning the chicken, stirring the leek slices to make sure they don't burn. Preheat the oven to 325°F.

3. Add the garlic and stir it for 1 minute. Add the wine, raise the heat to medium-high, and reduce the wine for 1 or 2 minutes. Add

(continued)

the tomatoes, stock, 1 teaspoon of salt, and pepper to taste. Bring to a simmer, then cover and bake until the chicken is tender, about 1½ hours.

4. In a stockpot, bring 5 quarts of water to a boil and add 1 tablespoon of salt and the vegetable oil. Cover and keep at a simmer so that it will be ready when the chicken is done.

5. When the chicken is tender, remove it to a platter, rub it with the remaining tablespoon of butter, and sprinkle with the parsley. Place it in a warm oven, with the heat off, until ready to serve as a main course after the pasta.

6. Add the fusilli to the boiling water, stir, and cook until al dente. Drain thoroughly. While the pasta is cooking, put the casserole over high heat and reduce the sauce until it has thickened. Set aside ½ cup of the sauce to serve with the chicken.

7. Toss the pasta in the sauce (reheated if necessary) in the casserole. Serve in heated bowls with a bowl of freshly grated Parmesan on the side.

BRAISED BEEF WITH PENNE, DRIED MUSHROOMS, AND MARJORAM

As with the Chicken with Fusilli, Tomatoes, and Rosemary (page 237), the pasta here is served as a first course and the meat as a main course. You can be less conventional, however, and serve them together.

—— SERVES 6–8 ——

1 ounce dried porcini mushrooms

1 cup hot water

¼ cup olive oil

4 pounds boneless beef chuck, rolled and tied

1 large onion, finely chopped

1 carrot, peeled and finely chopped

1 celery stalk, finely chopped

2 cloves garlic, minced

1½ cups dry red wine

1 bay leaf

1 cup canned Italian tomatoes, drained, seeded, and chopped

1 cup Beef Stock (page 6)

1 teaspoon marjoram

Salt

2 tablespoons vegetable oil

1 pound penne rigate (ribbed penne)

Freshly ground pepper

½ cup freshly grated Parmesan, plus more for serving

½ cup chopped fresh parsley

1. In a small bowl, cover the mushrooms with the hot water and let soak for 1 hour. Remove the mushrooms from the liquid and mince. Strain the liquid through a sieve lined with several layers of cheesecloth. Set both aside.

(continued)

2. Preheat the oven to 325°F. In a large flameproof casserole, heat the olive oil over medium-high heat. Pat the meat dry, add it to the casserole, and brown on all sides. Set the meat aside on a plate.

3. There should be about 3 tablespoons of oil left in the casserole. Add the onion, carrot, and celery and sauté over medium-low heat until soft. Add the garlic for the last minute of cooking. Add the wine and reduce it for 1 minute over high heat.

4. Return the meat and any accumulated juices to the casserole. Add the mushrooms, mushroom liquid, bay leaf, tomatoes, stock, and marjoram. Bring to a simmer, then cover and bake until the meat is tender, about 2½ hours.

5. In a stockpot, bring 5 quarts of water to a boil and add 1 tablespoon of salt and the vegetable oil. Cover and keep at a simmer so that it will be ready when the meat is done.

6. When the meat is tender, remove to a heated platter, cover loosely with aluminum foil, and place in a warm oven, with the heat off, until ready to serve it as a main course.

7. Add the penne to the boiling water, stir, and cook until al dente. Drain thoroughly. While the pasta is cooking, put the casserole over high heat and reduce the sauce until it has thickened to the consistency of thick gravy. Add salt and pepper to taste. Reserve 1 cup of the sauce to serve with the beef.

8. Toss the pasta in the sauce remaining in the casserole. Add the Parmesan and parsley. Serve in heated bowls, with a bowl of freshly grated Parmesan on the side.

RISOTTO WITH FOUR CHEESES

—— SERVES 4-6 ——

2 cups Chicken Stock (page 5), diluted with 2 cups water

3 tablespoons butter

3 tablespoons vegetable oil

3 shallots, finely chopped

1½ cups Arborio rice

1 cup dry white wine

1 cup heavy cream

2 ounces Italian Fontina cheese, chopped

2 ounces goat cheese, chopped

2 ounces Gorgonzola cheese, chopped

½ cup freshly grated Parmesan

1. In a saucepan, bring the diluted stock to a boil and keep it at a low simmer.

2. In a large heavy skillet, heat the butter and oil over medium heat, being careful not to let the butter brown. When the foam begins to subside, add the shallots and sauté them carefully until they soften. Add the rice and continue cooking, stirring constantly, until it begins to look translucent.

3. Add ½ cup of the heated stock and continue stirring the rice. When the liquid has been absorbed, add another ½ cup of stock, stirring constantly, so that the rice does not stick to the bottom of the pan. Continue cooking the rice in this way for 15 minutes. Then add ½ cup of the wine. When the wine has been absorbed, add the remaining ½ cup of wine. Continue cooking the rice with the stock, adding ½ cup at a time. When the rice is about 3 minutes from being al dente (about 25 minutes from the time you began cooking the risotto), add the cream and cheeses and continue cooking until all the cheese has melted. Serve on heated plates.

RISOTTO MILANESE

Risotto cooked in this way should take no more than 25 to 30 minutes, depending on the rice used, the weight and quality of the skillet, and the level of heat. It is imperative that the liquid be added ½ cup at a time, and only after the liquid already in the pan has been absorbed. Water that has been brought to a simmer can be used if you run out of stock. When the rice is done, it should be firm but not crunchy, the sauce creamy.

—— SERVES 4–6 ——

2 cups Beef Stock (page 6) diluted with 2 cups water

5 tablespoons butter

2 tablespoons vegetable oil

3 tablespoons bone marrow

3 shallots, finely chopped

1 cup dry white wine

1½ cups Arborio rice

¼ teaspoon saffron, soaked in ¼ cup of the hot stock

Freshly ground pepper

⅓ cup freshly grated Parmesan, plus more for serving

1. In a saucepan, bring the diluted stock to a boil and keep it at a low simmer.

2. In a large heavy skillet, heat 3 tablespoons of the butter and the oil over medium heat, being careful not to let the butter brown. When the foam begins to subside, add the bone marrow and shallots and cook until the shallots soften. Add ½ cup of the wine and cook until it is almost completely reduced.

3. Add the rice to the skillet and cook, stirring constantly, until the rice begins to look translucent. Add ½ cup of the heated stock and continue stirring the rice. When the liquid has been absorbed, add another ½ cup of stock, stirring constantly, so that the rice does not stick to the bottom of the pan. Continue cooking the rice in this way for 20 minutes, then add the saffron, its soaking liquid, and the rest of the wine. When the wine has been absorbed, continue cooking, adding the stock, until the rice is done—cooked through, but al dente. Stir in the remaining 2 tablespoons of butter, pepper to taste, and the Parmesan. Taste for additional seasoning—the rice probably won't need salt. Serve on heated plates with a bowl of freshly grated Parmesan on the side.

RISOTTO WITH FRESH AND DRIED MUSHROOMS

This is a dish we first tasted at the wonderful Tuscan restaurant Il Buco in Rome. It is a creamy risotto that makes full use of fresh and dried mushrooms.

—— SERVES 4-6 ——

1 ounce dried porcini mushrooms

1 cup hot water

2 cups Chicken Stock (page 5), diluted with 2 cups water

3 tablespoons butter

3 tablespoons olive oil

3 shallots, finely chopped

1½ cups Arborio rice

½ pound fresh mushrooms, chopped

1 cup dry white wine

½ cup heavy cream

3 tablespoons freshly grated Parmesan, plus more for serving

Garnish: chopped fresh parsley

1. In a small bowl, cover the dried mushrooms with the hot water and let soak for 1 hour. Remove the mushrooms from the liquid, chop them, and put aside. Strain the liquid through a sieve lined with several layers of cheesecloth and reserve.

2. In a saucepan, bring the diluted stock to a boil and keep it at a low simmer.

3. In a large heavy skillet, heat the butter and oil over medium heat, being careful not to let the butter brown. When the foam begins to subside, add the shallots and sauté them carefully until they soften. Add the rice and continue cooking, stirring constantly, until the rice begins to look translucent.

4. Add ½ cup of the heated stock and continue stirring the rice. When the liquid has been absorbed, add another ½ cup of stock, stirring constantly, so that the rice does not stick to the bottom of the pan. Continue cooking the rice in this way for 10 minutes.

5. Add the chopped dried mushrooms, the fresh mushrooms, and ½ cup of the wine. When the wine has been absorbed, add the remaining ½ cup of wine. Now add the mushroom liquid, ½ cup at a time. Continue cooking the rice, stirring in the heated stock. When the rice is about 3 minutes from being done al dente (about 25 minutes from the time you began cooking the risotto), add the cream, and cook until the rice is creamy. Stir in the Parmesan, garnish with the chopped fresh parsley, and serve on heated plates with a bowl of freshly grated Parmesan on the side.

RISOTTO WITH SAUSAGE AND CREAM

—— SERVES 4–6 ——

6 hot Italian sausages

5 tablespoons butter

2 cups Chicken Stock (page 5), diluted with 2 cups water

3 tablespoons olive oil

3 shallots, finely chopped

1½ cups Arborio rice

1 cup heavy cream

Garnish: chopped fresh parsley and freshly grated Parmesan

1. In a large skillet, sauté the sausages in 2 tablespoons of the butter over medium heat until cooked, about 30 minutes, pricking them with a fork. Remove from the heat. When the sausages are cool enough to handle, remove the casings and place the meat in a bowl, breaking it up with a fork. Set aside. Leave the sausage fat in the skillet.

2. In a saucepan, bring the diluted stock to a boil and keep it at a low simmer.

3. In the skillet, heat the remaining 3 tablespoons of the butter and the oil over medium heat, being careful not to let the butter brown. When the foam begins to subside, add the shallots and sauté them carefully until they soften. Add the rice and continue cooking, stirring constantly, until the rice begins to look translucent.

4. Add ½ cup of the heated stock and continue stirring the rice. When the liquid has been absorbed, add another ½ cup of stock, stirring constantly, so that the rice doesn't stick to the bottom of the pan. Continue cooking the rice in this way until the rice is nearly done, about 25 minutes.

5. Add the sausage meat and cream and continue cooking for another 3 minutes, allowing the cream to thicken and be partially absorbed by the rice. The sauce should be rich and creamy. Serve on heated plates, garnished with the chopped fresh parsley, with a bowl of freshly grated Parmesan on the side.

RISOTTO WITH RADICCHIO

— SERVES 4–6 —

5 tablespoons butter

1 cup roughly chopped radicchio

2 cups Chicken Stock (page 5), diluted with 2 cups water

3 tablespoons olive oil

3 shallots, finely chopped

1½ cups Arborio rice

1 cup dry white wine

3 tablespoons freshly grated Parmesan, plus more for garnish

1. In a large heavy skillet, melt 2 tablespoons of the butter, add the radicchio, and sauté over medium heat for 1 minute. Remove to a bowl.

2. In a saucepan, bring the diluted stock to a boil and keep it at a low simmer.

3. In the skillet, heat the remaining 3 tablespoons of butter and the oil over medium heat, being careful not to let the butter brown. When the foam begins to subside, add the shallots and sauté them carefully until they soften. Add the rice and continue cooking, stirring constantly, until the rice begins to look translucent.

4. Add ½ cup of the heated stock and continue stirring the rice. When the liquid has been absorbed, add another ½ cup of stock, stirring constantly, so that the rice does not stick to the bottom of the pan. Continue cooking the rice in this way for 15 minutes. Then add ½ cup of the wine. When the wine has been absorbed, add the remaining ½ cup of wine. When that has been absorbed, continue cooking the rice, stirring in the stock, ½ cup at a time. When the rice is about 3 minutes from being done (about 25 minutes from the time you began cooking the risotto), add the reserved radicchio and cook until it has heated through, no more than 1 or 2 minutes. Stir in the grated Parmesan and serve on heated plates with a bowl of freshly grated Parmesan on the side.

RISOTTO WITH SWEETBREADS AND BROWN BUTTER

— SERVES 4–6 —

1½ pounds sweetbreads

4 tablespoons lemon juice

1 teaspoon salt

13 tablespoons butter

3 tablespoons capers

3 tablespoons olive oil

¼ cup cognac

2 cups Chicken Stock (page 5), diluted with 2 cups water

3 shallots, finely chopped

1½ cups Arborio rice

1 cup dry white wine

1 cup heavy cream

Garnish: chopped fresh parsley

1. Soak the sweetbreads in cold water for 2 hours in the refrigerator. Drain. In a saucepan, cover the sweetbreads with fresh cold water, add 1 tablespoon of the lemon juice and the salt, and bring to a boil. Simmer for 15 minutes. Drain and immediately refresh under cold water for 5 minutes. Carefully remove the membrane covering the sweetbreads and chop the sweetbreads into 1-inch cubes.

2. In a small saucepan, melt 8 tablespoons of the butter over low heat until it turns a dark, nutty brown. Remove the saucepan from the heat and let the milk solids settle to the bottom of the pan; then pour off the clear butter into a bowl, leaving behind the dark sediment. In another saucepan, reduce the remaining 3 tablespoons of lemon juice and the capers slightly, then remove from the heat. Pour the clarified butter into the saucepan with the lemon juice and the capers and set aside.

3. In a heavy skillet, melt 2 tablespoons of the butter and 1 tablespoon of the oil and sauté the sweetbreads until they are golden brown. Add the cognac, bring to a boil, reduce by about half, and remove from the heat.

4. In a saucepan, bring the diluted stock to a boil and keep it at a low simmer.

5. In a large heavy skillet, heat the remaining 3 tablespoons of butter and the remaining oil over medium heat, being careful not to let the butter brown. When the foam begins to subside, add the shallots and sauté them carefully until they just soften. Add the rice and continue cooking, stirring constantly, until the rice begins to look translucent.

6. Add ½ cup of the heated stock and continue stirring the rice. When the liquid has been absorbed, add another ½ cup of stock, stirring constantly, so that the rice does not stick to the bottom of the pan. Continue cooking the rice in this way for 15 minutes. Then add ½ cup of the wine. When the wine has been absorbed, add the remaining ½ cup of wine. Continue cooking the rice, stirring in ½ cup of the heated stock at a time. When the rice is about 3 minutes from being al dente (about 25 minutes from the time you began cooking the risotto), add the cream and continue cooking until it thickens.

7. Quickly heat the sweetbreads and the butter/lemon/caper mixture and fold into the rice. Serve on heated plates and garnish with the chopped fresh parsley.

RISOTTO WITH SMOKED SALMON

—— SERVES 4-6 ——

2 cups Chicken Stock (page 5), diluted with 2 cups water

3 tablespoons butter

3 tablespoons olive oil

3 shallots, finely chopped

1½ cups Arborio rice

1 cup dry white wine

½ cup heavy cream

½ pound smoked salmon, chopped

Garnish: chopped fresh parsley

1. In a saucepan, bring the diluted stock to a boil and keep it at a low simmer.

2. In a large heavy skillet, heat the butter and oil over medium heat, being careful not to let the butter brown. When the foam begins to subside, add the shallots and sauté them carefully until they soften. Add the rice and continue to cook, stirring constantly, until the rice begins to look translucent.

3. Add ½ cup of the heated stock and continue stirring the rice. When the liquid has been absorbed, add another ½ cup of stock, stirring constantly, so that the rice does not stick to the bottom of the pan. Continue cooking the rice in this way for 15 minutes and then add ½ cup of the wine. When the wine has been absorbed add the remaining ½ cup of wine, and when it has been absorbed add the cream and the smoked salmon. Cook for a minute or two, until the salmon has heated through and the rice is creamy and cooked al dente. Serve on heated plates and garnish with a sprinkling of the chopped fresh parsley.

RISOTTO WITH ASPARAGUS

Because of the richness of the sauce, in this risotto the rice is boiled instead of being prepared in the usual way.

— SERVES 6 —

1 pound asparagus, peeled and trimmed, leaving only the top 4 inches

¼ pound mozzarella cheese

1 cup heavy cream

Salt

1 cup Arborio rice

8 tablespoons butter

½ cup freshly grated Parmesan, plus more for serving

Freshly ground pepper

Garnish: chopped fresh parsley

1. Cook the asparagus in boiling water for 40 minutes, or until it is very soft. Drain the asparagus, put it in a bowl, and shred it with a fork. Set aside.

2. Grate the mozzarella or chop it in a food processor and set aside. In a chilled bowl, whip the cream until it holds stiff peaks and place it in the refrigerator until ready to use.

3. Start to cook the rice 30 minutes before you wish to eat. In a saucepan, bring 2½ cups of water to a boil and add 1 teaspoon of salt. Stir in the rice, bring the water to a boil, cover, lower the heat, and simmer until the rice is tender, about 20 minutes.

4. While the rice is cooking, melt the butter in a saucepan, add the shredded asparagus, and cook until the asparagus begins to disintegrate, 10 to 15 minutes. Keep the mixture warm until the rice is cooked.

5. When the rice is done, place it in a serving bowl and immediately stir in the mozzarella, so it melts. Then add the asparagus/butter mixture and the Parmesan. Finally, fold in the whipped cream, add salt and pepper to taste, and serve on heated plates. Garnish with the chopped fresh parsley and serve with a bowl of freshly grated Parmesan on the side.

ACCOMPANIMENTS

This is a miscellaneous group of recipes that may accompany other dishes in the cookbook, or be consumed with each other, or even eaten by themselves. The green salads go well with any of the soups, stews, or pastas. The chutneys, raitas, and Aromatic Rice are intended to be served with the curries, but they are also delicious with less exotic stews. There are other dishes that make very appealing first courses—Crostini, Caponata, and Roasted Red Peppers and Anchovies, for example. And others may be served as hors d'oeuvres with drinks—Hummus, Baba Ghanouj, and Tapenade. You might even want to serve a combination of these accompaniments as a kind of international smorgasbord—Potato Salad, Pipérade, Tabbouleh, Cucumber and Red Onion Salad.

However you decide to use these recipes, they will provide you with a great deal of flexibility in preparing your menus.

SPICED BEEF

This unique hors d'oeuvre—a sirloin roast (use fillet if it has been a good year) dry-marinated for one or two weeks in brown spices, cooked until medium-rare, and sliced as thin as possible (paper-thin if you have a meat slicer) like the Italian cured beef called bresaola—is perfect for a large cocktail party. This marinated roast also makes a most elegant first course. The recipe comes to us by way of two of Princeton's most accomplished gourmets, Lynne Fagles and Betty Fussell.

— SERVES 20 —

One 6-pound sirloin roast, boned and rolled

⅓ cup brown sugar

¼ teaspoon ground cloves

1 teaspoon allspice

1 teaspoon mace

2 tablespoons freshly ground black pepper

1 teaspoon dried thyme

1 teaspoon ground coriander seeds

5 cardamom seeds

⅓ cup finely ground salt

Suet to cover the roast

1. Rub the roast with all the spices except the salt and place it in a glass or ceramic dish. Cover with aluminum foil and refrigerate for 2 days.

2. Rub the roast with the salt and return to the refrigerator for at least 7 days—14 days is better. Turn the meat once a day.

3. Preheat the oven to 350°F. Roast the beef for 1½ hours, covered with the suet or some other fat. Let the meat cool and slice it very thin.

COLD LAMB SALAD

This is an excellent way to use your leftover leg of lamb—
as a first course or a light lunch.

1 tablespoon Dijon mustard

1 tablespoon dry white wine

Salt and freshly ground pepper

1 teaspoon soy sauce

½ teaspoon ground cumin

3 scallions, with 1 inch of
green, finely chopped

2 tablespoons sherry vinegar

½ cup olive oil

12 thin slices cold leg of lamb

Garnish: chopped cilantro

1. In a mixing bowl, combine all the ingredients except the lamb and whisk until the dressing is emulsified.

2. Place 3 slices of cold lamb on each of 4 plates and pour the dressing in equal portions over each of the pieces. Garnish with the chopped cilantro and serve.

SALADE LYONNAISE

We sampled this delicious salad at the famous New York City restaurant La Caravelle. The recipe that follows is a variation on the one given to us by the owners, Robert Meyzen and Roger Fessaguet.

— SERVES 6 —

½ head romaine lettuce

½ head Boston lettuce

½ head chicory

3 tablespoons white wine vinegar

6 tablespoons olive oil

½ teaspoon prepared mustard

Salt and freshly ground pepper

4 slices of bacon, julienned

4 chicken livers, diced

1 endive, cut into ½-inch slices

3 very thin slices of onion, broken up

Croutons (one-fourth of the recipe on page 35)

1 tablespoon finely chopped fresh chives

1. Wash the lettuce and chicory. Drain in a colander and shake out excess moisture or dry in a salad spinner. Wrap the greens in paper towels, put in a plastic bag, and refrigerate for 1 to 2 hours.

2. In a small bowl, combine 1 tablespoon of the vinegar, the oil, mustard, and salt and freshly ground pepper to taste. Mix the vinaigrette well and set aside.

3. In a skillet, sauté the bacon until crisp, then remove it with a slotted spoon to drain on paper towels. Sauté the chicken livers in the bacon fat until they just turn from pink and remove them with a slotted spoon to drain on paper towels.

4. Over medium heat, deglaze the pan with the remaining 2 tablespoons vinegar, reduce it slightly, stir in the vinaigrette, and remove from the heat.

5. In a large salad bowl, mix the salad greens and endive and add the warm dressing. Mix well and garnish with the onion slices, croutons, chicken livers, bacon, and chives. Serve immediately.

MIXED SALAD WITH BLACKBERRIES, WALNUTS, AND GORGONZOLA DRESSING

This salad appeals to the senses in the way Bergman appealed to Bogart in Casablanca. *Serve it on a special summer night, with a sauterne or a late-harvest California white wine.*

—— SERVES 6 ——

1 head Bibb lettuce

1 bunch arugula

1 head radicchio

1 Belgian endive

1 teaspoon Dijon mustard

1 egg yolk

1 clove garlic, minced

Salt and freshly ground pepper

2 tablespoons balsamic vinegar

6 tablespoons olive oil

1 tablespoon heavy cream

3 tablespoons Gorgonzola cheese

½ cup walnuts

½ pint blackberries

1. Wash the Bibb lettuce, arugula (break off its thick stems and discard), radicchio, and endive. Be particularly careful with the arugula, as it is apt to be sandy. Drain in a colander and shake out the excess moisture or dry in a salad spinner. Wrap the greens in paper towels, put in a plastic bag, and refrigerate for 1 or 2 hours.

2. In a bowl large enough to contain the salad, beat the mustard into the egg yolk. Mix in the garlic, salt and pepper to taste, vinegar, and oil. Add the cream and Gorgonzola and beat until the mixture is almost smooth.

3. Add the salad to the bowl and toss with the dressing. On appropriate plates—clear cranberry-colored plates, for example—arrange the different leaves, sprinkle walnuts and blackberries over the top, and serve.

GOAT CHEESE AND SPINACH SALAD WITH WARM VINAIGRETTE

— SERVES 6 —

¾ pound Bucheron (or other French goat cheese)

1½ pounds spinach

1 shallot, minced

1 teaspoon Dijon mustard

¼ teaspoon dried basil

¼ teaspoon sugar

¼ teaspoon salt

Freshly ground pepper

3 tablespoons red wine vinegar

½ cup olive oil

1. Several hours before serving, remove the Bucheron from the refrigerator (it should be very cold). Pull off the skin that encircles the cheese. With a sharp knife, cut the Bucheron into 6 slices and place on a large plate. Cover with plastic wrap and let stand at room temperature until ready to assemble the salad. (If the edges crumble a bit, don't worry—put the crumbled cheese aside with the slices.)

2. Wash the spinach in a sink filled with cold water, pulling the stems off the leaves. Drain in a colander and dry thoroughly with paper towels. Tear the leaves into pieces and set aside in a salad bowl.

3. Combine the shallot, mustard, basil, sugar, salt, pepper to taste, vinegar, and oil in a small bowl and reserve.

4. When ready to serve, toss the spinach with 3 tablespoons of the vinaigrette—enough to barely coat the leaves. Arrange the spinach on 6 salad plates and arrange a slice of cheese on top of each bed of spinach.

5. In a small saucepan, warm the remaining vinaigrette over medium heat. As it comes just to a simmer, drizzle it in equal portions over the cheese and spinach. Serve immediately.

BIBB, WATERCRESS, PEPPER, AND ENDIVE SALAD WITH EGG LEMON DRESSING

— SERVES 6-8 —

1 teaspoon Dijon mustard

¼ teaspoon dried tarragon

1 small clove garlic, minced

¼ teaspoon sugar

Salt and freshly ground pepper

1 egg yolk

2 tablespoons lemon ju.

½ cup olive oil

1 head Bibb lettuce

1 bunch watercress

2 Belgian endives

½ red bell pepper, julienned

1. In a small bowl, combine the mustard, tarragon, garlic, sugar, and salt and pepper to taste. Mix well. Blend in the egg yolk and the lemon juice.

2. With a small whisk or a fork, beat the oil in very gradually. Set aside.

3. Wash the Bibb lettuce and watercress in a sink filled with cold water. Break off the thicker stems of the watercress and discard. Drain in a colander and shake off the excess moisture or dry the greens in a salad spinner. Wrap in paper towels, put in a plastic bag, and refrigerate for 1 hour or so to refresh.

4. Cut the endives in half lengthwise. Then cut each half lengthwise into ¹⁄₁₆-inch strips.

5. Place the endives, red pepper, Bibb, and watercress in a salad bowl and toss with the dressing.

ARUGULA, MUSHROOM, GRATED ZUCCHINI, AND CARROT SALAD WITH BALSAMIC VINAIGRETTE

We are very fond of balsamic vinegar, particularly with the slightly bitter taste of arugula, but not everyone likes its dense, sweet taste. If you are one of the latter, a good red or white wine vinegar may be substituted. Beating the oil in slowly makes for a fully integrated dressing.

—— SERVES 6–8 ——

1 teaspoon Dijon mustard

¼ teaspoon dried basil

1 small clove garlic, minced

Salt and freshly ground pepper

2 tablespoons balsamic
   vinegar

½ cup olive oil

2 bunches arugula

1 small zucchini

1 carrot, peeled

6 fresh mushrooms, finely
   sliced

1. In a small bowl, combine the mustard, basil, garlic, and salt and pepper to taste and blend in the vinegar.

2. With a small whisk or a fork, beat the oil in very gradually. Taste before you've added all the oil—vinegars are of varying strength and refinement and, accordingly, demand more or less oil.

3. Wash the arugula in a sink filled with cold water. It is apt to be sandy and may need two washings. Break off the thicker stems and discard. Drain in a colander and shake off the excess moisture or dry in a salad spinner. Wrap in paper towels, put in a plastic bag, and refrigerate for 1 hour or so.

4. Grate the zucchini and carrot in a food processor or cut into a very fine julienne by hand.

5. Place the mushrooms, grated zucchini and carrot, and arugula in a salad bowl and toss with the vinaigrette.

BIBB, WATERCRESS, WALNUT, OLIVE, AND GRUYÈRE SALAD WITH CREAMY WALNUT DRESSING

— SERVES 6 —

2 teaspoons Dijon mustard

1 small clove garlic, minced

¼ teaspoon salt

¼ teaspoon sugar

Freshly ground pepper

¼ teaspoon dried tarragon

1 tablespoon white wine vinegar

2 tablespoons heavy cream

5 tablespoons walnut oil

1 head Bibb lettuce

1 bunch watercress

½ cup walnuts, chopped

½ cup pitted and sliced Kalamata olives

¼ pound Swiss Gruyère cheese, julienned

1. In a small bowl, combine the mustard, garlic, salt, sugar, pepper to taste, and tarragon and blend in the vinegar.

2. With a small whisk or a fork, beat in the cream and then the walnut oil very gradually. Set the dressing aside.

3. Wash the Bibb lettuce and watercress in a sink filled with cold water. Break off and discard the thicker stems of the watercress. Drain in a colander and shake off the excess moisture or dry in a salad spinner. Wrap in paper towels, put in a plastic bag, and refrigerate for 1 to 2 hours.

4. Put the walnuts, olives, and Gruyère in a salad bowl, add the lettuce and watercress, and toss with the dressing.

BOSTON LETTUCE, ORANGE, AND AVOCADO SALAD WITH CURRIED LEMON DRESSING

— SERVES 6–8 —

½ teaspoon Dijon mustard

½ teaspoon curry powder

¼ teaspoon sugar

¼ teaspoon salt

1 small clove garlic, minced

2 tablespoons lemon juice

½ cup safflower oil

2 heads Boston lettuce

1 navel orange

1 small red onion, cut in half and sliced very thin

¼ cup chopped cilantro

1 medium avocado

1. In a small bowl, combine the mustard, curry powder, sugar, salt, and garlic and blend in the lemon juice.

2. With a small whisk or a fork, beat the oil in very gradually. Set aside.

3. Wash the lettuce in a sink filled with cold water. Drain in a colander and shake out the excess moisture or dry in a salad spinner. Wrap the lettuce in paper towels, put in a plastic bag, and refrigerate for 1 to 2 hours.

4. Cut off the first ½ inch of the orange from the stem end and discard. Then cut into ¼-inch slices. Remove the peel from the slices, remove the white pith, and separate into triangular pieces. Set aside.

5. Tear the lettuce into pieces and place in a salad bowl. Add the onion, orange, and cilantro. Slice the avocado into the bowl. Toss with the dressing and serve.

CELERY, MUSHROOM, AND EMMENTHALER SALAD

We first had this salad at Ristorante Ranieri in Rome.
Followed by a pasta, it makes a perfect Sunday supper.
Be sure to use imported Swiss cheese.

— SERVES 6 —

4 stalks celery, peeled to
  remove strings and julienned

½ pound fresh mushrooms,
  very thinly sliced

½ pound Emmenthaler
  cheese, cut into fine julienne
  strips

Juice of ½ lemon

⅓ cup green olive oil

Salt and freshly ground pepper

In a salad bowl, place the celery, mushrooms, and cheese. Toss with the lemon juice and oil, and add salt and pepper to taste. Serve immediately.

RED CABBAGE SALAD
WITH CURRIED VINAIGRETTE

—— SERVES 6 ——

1 small head red cabbage,
    quartered, cored, and cut
    into ¼-inch slices

1 small red onion, quartered
    and thinly sliced

¼ cup balsamic vinegar

1 tablespoon ketchup

1 teaspoon curry powder

1 clove garlic, minced

½ teaspoon Dijon mustard

Salt and freshly ground pepper

½ cup peanut oil

1. In a large serving bowl combine the cabbage and red onion.

2. In a small mixing bowl, combine the vinegar, ketchup, curry powder, garlic, mustard, and salt and pepper to taste. With a small whisk or fork beat in the oil very gradually. Pour the dressing over the cabbage, toss well, and refrigerate, covered, for 3 or 4 hours before serving.

CUCUMBER AND RED ONION SALAD

This sweet-and-sour salad should be made a day ahead of time to give the flavors a chance to develop fully. It is a summer favorite, but is also good in the winter with almost any stew.

— SERVES 6 —

2 cucumbers, peeled and very
    thinly sliced

Salt

1 cup cider vinegar

¼ cup sugar

½ red onion, cut in half and
    thinly sliced

Garnish: chopped fresh dill

1. In a colander, place the cucumber slices one layer at a time, lightly salting each layer. Put a plate weighted with a heavy object on top of the slices, then place the colander over a bowl to catch the water that drains from the cucumbers. Refrigerate.

2. In a saucepan, heat the vinegar, sugar, and red onion over low heat until the sugar dissolves—this shouldn't take more than 2 or 3 minutes. Transfer to a serving bowl, cool, and refrigerate.

3. Remove the cucumbers from the refrigerator and rinse them under cold water. Pat them dry with paper towels and add to the onion mixture. Refrigerate, covered, for at least 3 more hours.

4. Drain the cucumbers and onion, reserving 5 tablespoons of the liquid. Toss the cucumbers with the reserved liquid and garnish with the chopped fresh dill.

POTATO SALAD

— SERVES 8 —

3 pounds small red potatoes

3 tablespoons olive oil

1 tablespoon balsamic vinegar

Salt and freshly ground pepper

3 celery stalks, chopped

1 large red onion, chopped

1 red pepper, chopped

2 hard-boiled eggs, chopped

5 tablespoons finely chopped fresh dill

6 tablespoons mayonnaise

1 tablespoon Dijon mustard

1. In a saucepan, boil the potatoes in salted water for 20 minutes, or until just tender. Let cool and rub off their skins. Cut into quarters, or whatever shape you prefer.

2. In a large bowl, combine the oil, vinegar, and salt and pepper to taste. Mix well. Add the potatoes and toss carefully with your hands (you don't want to break up the potatoes), making sure they are well coated. Without mixing, add the celery, red onion, red pepper, eggs, and dill.

3. In a small bowl, combine the mayonnaise and mustard and add it to the potato salad, again mixing carefully with your hands to maintain the shape of the potatoes. Combine all the ingredients thoroughly and refrigerate, covered, for 3 hours.

RICE SALAD

A few years ago, during the summer we spent in the Umbrian town of Umbertide, we often served this dish for lunch, accompanied by a bottle of the simple, local white wine. Colorful and delicious, this salad is great for a midsummer lunch wherever you are, which is not to say it can't be served any time of the year.

—— SERVES 12 ——

Salt

2 cups long-grain rice

½ cup olive oil

⅓ cup lemon juice

5 tablespoons Dijon mustard

1 cup fresh peas

3 red peppers, peeled, cored, and julienned

3 tomatoes, peeled, seeded, and chopped

1 medium red onion, quartered and thinly sliced

5 tablespoons chopped parsley

20 cornichons, roughly chopped

¾ pound black olives (Kalamata or Gaeta), pitted and sliced

¾ pound green olives (Sicilian or Spanish), pitted and sliced

½ pound smoked Virginia ham, julienned

Freshly ground pepper

1. In a large saucepan, bring 3 cups of salted water to a boil, add the rice, and stir to distribute. Lower the heat and simmer, covered, for 15 to 20 minutes, or until the water has been completely absorbed and the rice is cooked al dente.

2. Spread the rice on a baking sheet lined with paper towels and allow it to cool and dry.

3. In a mixing bowl, beat together the oil, lemon juice, and mustard until completely combined. Set aside.

4. In a large serving bowl, combine the rice with the remaining ingredients. Toss a few times with your hands to distribute. Add the dressing and toss again, until everything is well coated. Refrigerate, covered, for 2 to 3 hours, add salt and pepper to taste, and serve.

PANZANELLA

*A Roman dish, panzanella is a bread salad that is served in
as many different versions as there are those who make it. This recipe
is based on the panzanella served in the Roman restaurant
La Fontanella.*

—— SERVES 6 ——

½ red onion, cut in half and thinly sliced

3 celery stalks, quartered lengthwise and cut into 1-inch slices

1 cucumber, peeled, seeded, and diced

4 tomatoes, peeled, seeded, and chopped

2 tablespoons capers

3 tablespoons chopped fresh parsley

1 loaf day-old Italian bread

¾ cup olive oil

¼ cup red wine vinegar

2 tablespoons lemon juice

2 cloves garlic, finely minced

Salt and freshly ground pepper

1. In a large serving bowl, combine the red onion, celery, cucumber, tomatoes, capers, and parsley and toss a few times to mix.

2. Cut the bread into 1-inch slices, remove the crusts, and tear the bread into small chunks. Add the bread to the bowl and toss once or twice.

3. In a small bowl, combine the oil, vinegar, lemon juice, and garlic and pour the dressing over the bread mixture. Toss and let the salad stand for 1 hour to allow the bread to absorb the dressing. When you're ready to serve the salad, add salt and pepper to taste and toss well.

TABBOULEH

A refreshing Middle Eastern salad, tabbouleh is good with just about anything. Certainly it is a perfect accompaniment to any of the Indian, Middle Eastern, or North African dishes we have included, such as Chicken Tagine with Prunes, Onions, and Almonds (page 94), Eggplant and Ground Lamb in Yogurt (page 140), or Saag Gosht (page 117). It is also satisfying just by itself.

—— SERVES 6 ——

1½ cups fine bulgur wheat

2 cups chopped flat-leaf parsley

2 cups chopped curly-leaf parsley

½ cup chopped fresh mint

3 scallions, with 2 inches of green, finely sliced

3 medium tomatoes, peeled, seeded, and chopped

½ cup lemon juice

2 cloves garlic, minced

2 teaspoons white wine vinegar

½ cup olive oil

½ teaspoon ground cumin

1 tablespoon salt

Freshly ground pepper

1. In a large bowl, cover the bulgur wheat with boiling water and let stand for 1 hour.

2. Drain the bulgur wheat in a large sieve, place it in a dish towel, and squeeze out the excess liquid.

3. In a large bowl, combine both parsleys, the mint, scallions, tomatoes, lemon juice, garlic, vinegar, oil, cumin, salt, and pepper to taste and mix well. Add the bulgur wheat and toss until thoroughly combined. Refrigerate, covered, for at least 3 hours, although overnight is best.

CAPONATA

*We've used balsamic vinegar and sultanas to achieve the
traditional sweet-and-sour taste of this dish. It is marvelous as
part of an antipasto, alone as a first course, or, lukewarm, as an
accompaniment to roast lamb.*

— SERVES 6 —

2 medium unpeeled eggplants,
   cut into 1-inch cubes

Salt and freshly ground pepper

2 sweet peppers, preferably
   red, cored, seeded, and cut
   into 1-inch pieces

6 celery stalks, each cut into
   quarters lengthwise and
   then into 1-inch lengths

1 large onion, chopped

1½ cups canned Italian
   tomatoes, drained, seeded,
   and chopped

½ cup balsamic vinegar

⅔ cup olive oil

3 cloves garlic, minced

½ cup golden raisins

½ cup pitted and halved
   green olives (Sicilian)

2 tablespoons capers,
   drained

2 bay leaves

1. In a colander, toss the eggplant cubes generously with salt and
let the eggplant drain for 1 hour. Rinse with cold water and dry
with paper towels, pressing gently to remove the excess liquid.

2. Preheat the oven to 325°F.

3. In a large mixing bowl, combine the eggplant, peppers, celery,
onion, and tomatoes.

4. In a small bowl, blend the vinegar, oil, and garlic. Add the
mixture to the vegetables and toss. Stir in the sultanas, olives,
and capers.

5. Place the vegetable mixture in a large Pyrex baking dish
(approximately 15 x 10 x 3 inches). Bury the bay leaves in the

mixture and cover with aluminum foil. Bake for 30 minutes. Remove the foil and bake until the vegetables are very tender, another 1½ hours, stirring occasionally. Let the mixture cool, remove the bay leaves, and add salt and pepper to taste. Serve at room temperature.

EGGPLANT SALAD

1 medium eggplant

3 cups plain yogurt

3 shallots, finely chopped

3 tablespoons finely chopped fresh mint

Salt and freshly ground pepper

½ teaspoon cumin seeds, toasted and ground*

1 clove garlic, minced

1 tomato, peeled, seeded, and chopped

½ teaspoon paprika

2 tablespoons lemon juice

---

* To toast cumin seeds, place them in a hot skillet (do not add oil or butter) and cook them over medium heat, stirring constantly, until they are brown, about 5 minutes. Grind with a mortar and pestle.

1. Preheat the oven to 400°F.

2. Make several slashes, about 2 inches long, in the skin of the eggplant. Set the eggplant on a baking sheet and bake until tender, about 1 hour. When the eggplant is cool enough to handle, peel and chop it, and place in a serving bowl.

3. Add the yogurt, shallots, mint, salt and pepper to taste, cumin seeds, garlic, tomato, paprika, and lemon juice, mix well, and refrigerate until ready to serve.

PIPÉRADE

Neither fish nor fowl, this egg and vegetable dish comes from the Basque country of France. It is wonderful by itself for a light meal, or serve it following soup.

— SERVES 4 —

3 tablespoons olive oil

2 tablespoons butter

1 medium onion, cut in half and thinly sliced

1 clove garlic, minced

2 red peppers, chopped

2 tomatoes, peeled, seeded, and chopped

¼ teaspoon cayenne pepper

1 teaspoon chopped fresh basil (or ⅓ teaspoon dried basil)

Salt and freshly ground pepper

3 eggs

Garnish: chopped fresh parsley

1. In a large skillet, heat 1 tablespoon of the oil and 1 tablespoon of the butter and lightly brown the onion and garlic. Remove to a bowl.

2. Add 1 tablespoon of the oil and the remaining tablespoon of butter to the skillet and lightly brown the red peppers. Place them in the bowl with the onion.

3. In the remaining tablespoon of oil, cook the tomatoes until they have softened and their liquid has reduced to about 1 tablespoon. Return the onion, garlic, and peppers to the skillet, add the cayenne, basil, and salt and pepper to taste, and cook over medium heat, stirring gently to prevent the vegetables from scorching, for about 5 minutes.

4. Reduce the heat to low, beat the eggs in a bowl, and stir them into the vegetables gently. Cook the eggs until they have just set. Serve immediately, garnished with the chopped fresh parsley.

ROASTED RED PEPPERS
AND ANCHOVIES

Roasted peppers make a sublime first course before pasta. We often serve them as part of an extravagant antipasto—including Caponata (page 272), Italian cheeses and meats, and Italian tuna fish—with some crusty bread on hand to sop up the olive oil, which should be green and fruity. If you can find yellow bell peppers, which are even sweeter than the red, substitute them for half the red. If you can find neither, green peppers will do. We have discovered that the Italian anchovies that come packed in glass jars are in a class by themselves.

— SERVES 8 —

½ cup olive oil

2 cloves garlic, minced

½ teaspoon dried basil

10 red peppers

24 anchovy fillets (three 2-ounce tins), cut in half lengthwise

Freshly ground pepper

1. Preheat the oven to 450°F.

2. In a small bowl, blend the oil, garlic, and basil. Set aside.

3. Roast the peppers on a baking sheet until the skins are blistered and slightly charred, turning them once, about 15 minutes on each side.

4. Put the peppers in a paper bag, close the bag tightly, and let the peppers sit until they are cool enough to handle, about 15 minutes. Peel and core the peppers, remove the seeds, and cut the peppers into strips.

5. In a glass bowl, toss the peppers with the anchovies, oil mixture, and pepper to taste and let them stand at room temperature, covered, for 1 or 2 hours before serving.

CUCUMBER, GREEN PEPPER, AND YOGURT SALAD

— SERVES 4 —

3 tablespoons olive oil

1 tablespoon mustard seeds

1 green pepper, roasted and finely chopped

1 medium onion, finely chopped

1 teaspoon ground ginger

1 teaspoon sugar

½ teaspoon salt

2 cups plain yogurt

1 medium cucumber, peeled, seeded, and diced

Garnish: chopped cilantro or fresh mint

1. In a skillet, heat the oil over medium heat. Add the mustard seeds and lightly toast. When they start to pop, add the green pepper, onion, and ground ginger and continue cooking, stirring constantly, until the vegetables soften slightly but are not limp, about 5 minutes. Stir in the sugar and salt, remove from the heat, and let cool.

2. In a serving bowl, combine the yogurt, cucumber, and vegetable mixture, and mix well. Refrigerate, covered, for 3 hours. Garnish with the chopped cilantro or fresh mint and serve.

CUCUMBER RAITA

This is a traditional accompaniment to curries—the coolness of the yogurt tempers the heat of the spices.

— SERVES 6 —

1½ cups plain yogurt

½ cup sour cream

1 teaspoon cumin seeds, toasted and ground (see page 274)

½ teaspoon salt

2 cucumbers, peeled, cut into quarters lengthwise, seeded, and finely sliced

Garnish: chopped fresh mint

1. In a small bowl, blend the yogurt and sour cream. Stir in the cumin seeds and salt. Fold in the cucumbers. Refrigerate, covered, for 1 or 2 hours.

2. Stir the raita before serving and garnish with the chopped fresh mint.

EGGPLANT RAITA

Like the preceding recipe, this is to be served with curry. It is especially good with Saag Gosht (page 117) or any lamb curry.

— SERVES 8 —

1 large eggplant

¼ cup dried currants

½ cup boiling water

4 tablespoons vegetable oil

1 small onion, finely chopped

1 teaspoon salt

1½ cups plain yogurt

½ cup sour cream

2 teaspoons garam masala (see page 117)

Garnish: chopped cilantro

1. Preheat the oven to 400°F.

2. Make several slashes, about 2 inches long, in the skin of the eggplant. Set the eggplant on a baking sheet and bake until tender, about 1 hour. When it is cool enough to handle, peel the eggplant, chop the flesh, and set aside.

3. In a small bowl, cover the currants with the boiling water and let soak for 30 minutes. Drain and reserve.

4. In a skillet, heat the oil over medium-low heat, add the onion, and sauté until soft. Add the salt, stir, and sauté a few minutes more. Add the eggplant pieces and continue to cook for another 3 or 4 minutes, stirring.

5. In a serving bowl, blend the yogurt and sour cream, and when the eggplant mixture has cooled a bit, fold it into the yogurt, along with the garam masala and the currants.

6. Chill, covered, for 2 or 3 hours. Garnish with the chopped cilantro before serving.

AROMATIC RICE

We always serve this with curry, but it is also delicious with roast lamb or chicken.

— SERVES 8 —

3 cups Chicken Stock (page 5)

½ teaspoon saffron

3 tablespoons vegetable oil

1 teaspoon cumin seeds

1 small onion, chopped

3 cloves garlic, minced

6 cardamom pods

1 cinnamon stick

2 cups long-grain rice

⅓ cup vermicelli, broken into ½-inch pieces

2 bay leaves

1 teaspoon salt

1. Preheat the oven to 400°F.

2. In a saucepan, bring the stock to a boil, turn off the heat, and add the saffron. Let it steep while you prepare the rice.

3. In a medium flameproof casserole, heat the oil over medium heat. Add the cumin seeds and cook for 30 seconds.

4. Add the onion and sauté, stirring, until it begins to soften.

5. Add the garlic, cardamom pods, and cinnamon stick and sauté for 30 seconds.

6. Add the rice and vermicelli and sauté, stirring, until the rice is transparent.

7. Add the hot stock, the bay leaves, and the salt and bring to a boil.Cover and bake for 17 minutes.

8. Transfer to a warmed serving dish, remove the bay leaves, cinnamon stick, and cardamom pods, and serve.

APPLE AND PEAR CHUTNEY

3 carrots, peeled, cut in half lengthwise, and thinly sliced

3 green cooking apples, peeled, cored, and chopped

2 pears, peeled, cored, and chopped

½ medium onion, chopped

1 green pepper, chopped

1 orange, quartered and thinly sliced, with peel

3 cups cider vinegar

2 cups dark brown sugar

1 teaspoon salt

1½ teaspoons cinnamon

½ teaspoon ground cloves

2 teaspoons ground ginger

½ teaspoon Tabasco sauce, or to taste

1. In a saucepan, combine all the ingredients and bring to a boil, stirring constantly. Lower the heat and simmer, stirring occasionally, for approximately 1 hour, until the liquid reduces to a syrup.

2. Let the chutney cool, transfer it to a bowl, and refrigerate, covered, for at least 3 hours before serving.

NECTARINE CHUTNEY

This is one of our favorite fruit chutneys. Like the preceding chutney, it goes with anything, particularly Chicken Tagine with Prunes, Onions, and Almonds (page 94), or any kind of curry dish. Or try it with a ham dinner—chutney is a very versatile condiment.

— MAKES 5 CUPS —

5 pounds nectarines

½ small onion, minced

1 clove garlic, minced

2 cups cider vinegar

2 tablespoons coarse salt

1 pound dark brown sugar

1 teaspoon ground cinnamon

1 teaspoon ground cloves

2 teaspoons dry mustard

½ cup chopped crystalized ginger

¼ teaspoon cayenne pepper

½ teaspoon allspice

1 lemon rind, julienned

1 cup slivered blanched almonds, chopped

1. Peel the nectarines by dropping them into boiling water for a few seconds to loosen their skins. Let cool and remove the skins. Cut the nectarines into chunks, discarding the pits.

2. In a large stockpot, add the skinned nectarines with the remaining ingredients except the almonds, and bring to a boil. Lower the heat and simmer, uncovered, stirring occasionally to prevent burning, until the chutney thickens, 1½ to 2 hours. Remove from the heat and stir in the almonds.

3. When the chutney is cool, transfer it to a bowl and refrigerate, covered, for at least 3 hours before serving.

TOMATO CHUTNEY

— MAKES 2 CUPS —

2½ cups canned Italian tomatoes, drained, seeded, and chopped

1 tablespoon grated fresh ginger

4 cloves garlic, minced

½ teaspoon red pepper flakes

1 teaspoon cumin seeds, toasted and ground (see page 274)

¾ cup granulated sugar

1 teaspoon salt

1 cup cider vinegar

¼ cup golden raisins

¼ cup chopped cilantro

1. In a large enameled flameproof casserole, bring the tomatoes, ginger, garlic, and red pepper flakes to a boil, then lower the heat and simmer, uncovered, for 30 minutes, stirring occasionally to prevent the mixture from burning.

2. Add the cumin seeds, sugar, salt, and vinegar and continue cooking at a low simmer, uncovered, until the mixture thickens, about 1 hour. Stir occasionally to prevent the chutney from sticking to the bottom of the casserole.

3. Add the golden raisins for the last 15 minutes of cooking. Remove from the heat, add the cilantro, and place in a glass or earthenware bowl. When the chutney is cool, refrigerate, covered, for at least 3 hours before serving.

HUMMUS

*Since the chickpeas are puréed in this Middle Eastern dish,
we find the convenience of the canned variety outweighs the
advantages of the texture of the dried.*

— MAKES 6 CUPS —

4 cups canned chick-peas,
    drained

½ cup tahini

4 cloves garlic, minced

½ cup lemon juice

¼ teaspoon ground cumin

1 teaspoon salt

¾ cup olive oil

Freshly ground pepper

¼ cup chopped fresh parsley

1. In a food processor, purée the chickpeas, tahini, garlic, lemon
juice, cumin, salt, and ½ cup of the olive oil.

2. With a rubber spatula, scrape down the sides of the bowl. With
the motor running, add the remaining oil to the purée.

3. Transfer to a bowl and add salt and pepper to taste. Stir in the
chopped fresh parsley and serve with warm pita bread.

BABA GHANOUJ

— MAKES 3 CUPS —

2 medium eggplants

3 cloves garlic, minced

¼ cup lemon juice

½ cup olive oil

½ cup tahini

½ teaspoon ground cumin

½ teaspoon salt

Freshly ground pepper

Garnish: chopped cilantro or parsley

1. Preheat the oven to 400°F.

2. Make several slashes, about 2 inches long, in the skin of the eggplants. Set the eggplants on a baking sheet and bake until tender, about 1 hour. When they are cool enough to handle, peel the eggplants, chop the flesh, and place in a bowl.

3. In a food processor, blend the garlic, lemon juice, oil, tahini, cumin, and salt for about 30 seconds, or until all the ingredients are thoroughly combined. Add the eggplant, discarding any juices that have accumulated in the bowl, and purée until smooth.

4. Spoon the purée into a bowl and add pepper to taste. Depending on the size of the eggplants and your own taste, you may want to add more lemon juice or salt. Garnish with the chopped cilantro or fresh parsley and serve with warm pita bread.

TAPENADE

A favorite Provençal dish, tapenade is an ideal dip for raw vegetables or pieces of French bread. It is also wonderful on toast points.

—— MAKES 1 CUP ——

1 cup black olives (Kalamatas work very well), pitted

One 2-ounce can anchovies, drained and rinsed well

3 tablespoons capers, drained and rinsed

Juice of 1 lemon

1 clove garlic, chopped

3 shallots, chopped

3 tablespoons mayonnaise

¼ cup olive oil

2 tablespoons finely chopped fresh basil

1. In a food processor, purée the olives, anchovies, capers, lemon juice, garlic, shallots, and mayonnaise until smooth.

2. With the motor running, add the oil in a thin stream until it is completely incorporated. Remove to a bowl and mix in the chopped fresh basil. Chill, covered, for 1 or 2 hours, or until ready to serve.

CROSTINI

This savory chicken liver dish may be served as a first course or as an hors d'oeuvre with drinks.

— SERVES 8 —

¾ pound chicken livers

6 tablespoons olive oil, plus more for garnishing toasts

1 small onion, very finely chopped

¾ teaspoon dried sage, crushed

4 anchovy fillets, chopped

2 cloves garlic, minced

1 teaspoon capers

2 teaspoons lemon juice

½ cup freshly grated Parmesan

Freshly ground pepper

24 thin slices of Italian bread

1. Preheat the oven to 450°F.

2. Remove the membranes from the chicken livers and dice the livers. In a large skillet, heat the oil over medium-low heat. Add the livers, onion, sage, and anchovies and cook, stirring occasionally, for 5 minutes. Add the garlic and capers and cook until the liver pieces are firm but still slightly pink inside, another 5 minutes.

3. Remove from the heat and mash the liver mixture with a wooden spoon. (We like some texture to remain, but if you prefer it very smooth, you may purée it in a food processor.) Add the lemon juice, Parmesan, and pepper to taste.

4. Place the bread on a baking sheet and toast in the oven for a few minutes on each side.

5. Spread the liver mixture generously on the toasted bread and put 2 or 3 drops of oil on each slice.

6. Return to the oven for 1 or 2 minutes, until heated through.

BISTRO APPETIZER

We sampled something like this dish in a small Paris bistro. It is a tangy little salad, attractive when placed on a small plate and served as part of a first course—as a sort of garnish to it.

— SERVES 4-6 —

1 lemon, juice and rind

4 tablespoons red wine vinegar

3½ teaspoons sugar

1 tablespoon salt

½ cup olive oil

1 teaspoon Dijon mustard

¼ teaspoon dried tarragon

1 teaspoon coriander seeds, toasted (follow directions for toasting cumin seeds on page 274)

½ pound small fresh mushrooms, quartered

3 tablespoons chopped pimientos

2 celery stalks, peeled to remove stringy outer part, very finely chopped

Freshly ground pepper

1. In a small saucepan, combine the lemon rind, water to cover (about 3 cups), 4 tablespoons of the vinegar, 3 teaspoons of the sugar, and the salt. Bring the liquid to a boil, then lower the heat and simmer for 1 hour. Remove the lemon rind and rinse it under cold running water, removing any flesh on the rind. Cut it into very fine julienne strips, about ½ inch long.

2. In a large bowl, place the lemon rind, 2 tablespoons of the lemon juice and ½ teaspoon of sugar, the oil, mustard, tarragon, coriander seeds, mushrooms, pimientos, and celery. Mix well and refrigerate, covered, for 5 hours, stirring occasionally.

3. When you are ready to serve, drain the mixture and reserve 1 or 2 tablespoons of the marinating liquid. Place the mixture in a serving bowl, sprinkle with the reserved liquid, and serve.

INDEX